THE BIBLE OF PESCATARIAN RECIPES

3 in 1

+150 Delicious Simple Seafood Recipes

Johan Castillo, Arthur Foster, Adriana Mayer

Disclaimer

The information contained i is meant to serve as a comprehensive collection of strategies that the author of this eBook has done research about. Summaries, strategies, tips and tricks are only recommendation by the author, and reading this eBook will not guarantee that one's results will exactly mirror the author's results. The author of the eBook has made all reasonable effort to provide current and accurate information for the readers of the eBook. The author and it's associates will not be held liable for any unintentional error or omissions that may be found. The material in the eBook may include information by third parties. Third party materials comprise of opinions expressed by their owners. As such, the author of the eBook does not assume responsibility or liability for any third party material or opinions. Whether because of the progression of the internet, or the unforeseen changes in company policy and editorial submission guidelines, what is stated as fact at the time of this writing may become outdated or inapplicable later.

Sommario

The Truly Healthy Pescatarian Cookbook

50 Fresh & Delicious Recipes

Adriana Mayer

Disclaimer

The information contained i is meant to serve as a comprehensive collection of strategies that the author of this eBook has done research about. Summaries, strategies, tips and tricks are only recommendation by the author, and reading this eBook will not guarantee that one's results will exactly mirror the author's results. The author of the eBook has made all reasonable effort to provide current and accurate information for the readers of the eBook. The author and it's associates will not be held liable for any unintentional error or omissions that may be found. The material in the eBook may include information by third parties. Third party materials comprise of opinions expressed by their owners. As such, the author of the eBook does not assume responsibility or liability for any third party material or opinions. Whether because of the progression of the internet, or the unforeseen changes in company policy and editorial submission guidelines, what is stated as fact at the time of this writing may become outdated or inapplicable later.

INTRODUCTION

A pescatarian diet is a flexible vegetarian diet that includes fish and other seafood. When you add fish to a vegetarian diet, you reap the following benefits:

Fish protein increases satiety as compared to beef and chicken. This means you will feel full quickly and not overeat. If you are looking to shed some pounds, it's the right time to start being on a pescatarian diet.

Calcium is extremely important for your bone health. Merely eating vegetables does not provide your body with enough calcium. But adding fish to a vegetarian diet does

Fatty fish are great sources of omega-3 fatty acids. These acids help lower inflammation in the body, which, in turn, reduces the risk of obesity, diabetes, and heart disease.

Compared to other animal proteins, consuming fish contributes lesser to greenhouse gas emission. So, you can protect the environment and your health.

For some, just eating vegetables, fruit, and nuts can be boring. Adding fish or any other seafood helps improve the taste and overall mood of lunch and/or dinner.

Many people are allergic to eggs, lactose intolerant, or may want to avoid eating meat or dairy products. For them, fish can be a good source of complete protein, calcium, and healthy fats.

WHAT DO PESCATARIANS EAT?

SEAFOOD: Mackerel, bass, haddock, salmon, tuna, Hilsa, sardines, Pomfret, carps, cod, caviar, mussels, crayfish, oyster, prawns, lobster, crab, squid, and scallops.

VEGETABLES: Spinach, chard, radish greens, carrot greens, Bengal gram greens, beetroot, carrot, broccoli, cauliflower, cabbage, Chinese cabbage, sweet potato, radish, turnip, parsnip, kale, cucumber, and tomato.

FRUITS: Apple, banana, avocado, strawberries, blackberries, mulberries, blueberries, gooseberries, pineapple, papaya, dragon fruit, passion fruit, watermelon, muskmelon, guava, peach, pear, pluot, plum, and mango.

PROTEIN: Kidney beans, lentils, fish, mushroom, Bengal gram, sprouts, black-eyed peas, cowpeas, garbanzo beans, soybean, soy milk, edamame, and tofu.

WHOLE GRAINS: Brown rice, barley, broken wheat, sorghum, multigrain bread, and multigrain flour.

FATS & OILS: Olive oil, avocado oil, fish oil, ghee, sunflower butter, and rice bran oil.

Nuts & Seeds Almonds, walnuts, pistachios, macadamia, pine nuts, hazelnuts, sunflower seeds, melon seeds, pumpkin seeds, chia seeds, and flaxseeds.

Herbs & Spices Cilantro, dill, fennel, parsley, oregano, thyme, bay leaf, chili flakes, chili powder, Kashmiri red chili powder, turmeric, coriander, cumin, mustard seeds, English mustard, mustard paste, star anise, saffron, cardamom, clove, garlic, cinnamon, ginger, mace, nutmeg, Allspice, onion powder, garlic powder, and ginger powder.

BEVERAGES: Water, coconut water, detox" water>, and freshly pressed fruit/vegetable juices.

With these ingredients, you can easily come up with a diet plan that's nutritionally balanced. Take a look at this sample pescatarian diet plan.

SEAFOOD SALAD

Servings:6

INGREDIENTS

- 300g orecchiette pasta
- 1 small eggplant, cut into 1cm pieces
- 1 red onion, cut into wedges
- 1 red capsicum, cut into 1cm pieces
- 2 garlic cloves, chopped
- 1/2 cup (125ml) extra virgin olive oil
- 250g punnet cherry tomatoes, halved
- 1/3 cup (80ml) white wine
- 500g pot-ready mussels
- 6 small squid, cleaned, cut into rings, tentacles reserved

- 1 tablespoon white wine vinegar
- 1 tablespoon chilli tomato paste
- 1/3 cup chopped flat-leaf parsley
- 1/4 cup (35g) chopped semi-dried tomatoes
- Rocket leaves, to serve

PREPARATION

Preheat the oven to 220 degrees Celsius and line a baking sheet with foil.

Drain and rehydrate the pasta according to the package directions.

Season the eggplant, onion, and capsicum with the garlic and 2 tablespoons oil. Cook for 15 minutes, or until just soft, on the lined baking tray. Cook for another 6-8 minutes, or until the tomatoes have softened.

Bring the wine to a boil in a large saucepan over medium-high heat. Cover with a lid and cook for 3 minutes, or until all of the mussels have opened. Remove the mussels from their shells, leaving a few for decoration.

In a wide frypan, heat 1 tablespoon of oil over high heat. Season the squid and fry for 1 minute, turning once, or until golden. Delete from the equation.

In a mixing bowl, combine the vinegar, tomato paste, and parsley with the remaining 65ml oil. It's that time of year. To eat, throw the seafood, roasted vegetables, semi-dried tomato, and rocket in a bowl with the dressing.

ROASTED SEAFOOD WITH LEMON AND HERBS

Servings:4

INGREDIENTS

- 8 scampi, halved, cleaned
- 8 large green prawns
- 8 scallops on the half shell
- 1/4 cup (60ml) olive oil
- 2 garlic cloves, finely chopped
- Finely grated zest and juice of 1 lemon, plus lemon wedges to serve
- 2 tablespoons chopped lemon thyme or thyme
- 2 tablespoons chopped flat-leaf parsley

PREPARATION

Preheat the oven to 200°C or 400°C if using a wood fired oven.

Arrange the seafood in a single layer in a large baking dish. Mix the oil, garlic, zest, juice, and thyme in a cup, then brush the mixture over the seafood and season. Bake for 10 minutes (or 5-7 minutes in the center of a woodfired oven) or until seafood is cooked. Serve with lemon wedges and a sprinkling of parsley.

SEAFOOD COCKTAIL OF KING PRAWN, AVOCADO AND BASIL

Servings:4

INGREDIENTS

- 1 carrot, peeled and diced
- 600g cooked king prawns, peeled and deveined
- 3 spring onions, thinly sliced (green part only)
- 1/2 cucumber, peeled, deseeded and diced into 5mm cubes
- 1 avocado, finely diced
- 2 tbs capers, coarsely chopped
- Grated zest of 1 lime
- 18g snow pea tendrils

- DRESSING
- 1 tbs lime juice
- 2 tbs verjuice
- 1 tbs mayonnaise
- 1 tbs olive oil
- 4 tbs fresh chopped basil

PREPARATION

To make the dressing, whisk together all of the ingredients (except the basil) in a mixing bowl. Put aside after seasoning with salt and pepper.

Cook carrot squares for 3 minutes in boiling water. Rinse in cold water after draining. 4 prawns are set aside and left whole. Combine the remaining prawns, carrots, spring onions, cucumber, avocado, capers, and lime zest in a mixing bowl.

FRUTTA DI MARE ALL'ACQUA PAZZA (SEAFOOD IN CRAZY WATER)

Servings:6

INGREDIENTS

- 1 cup (250ml) dry white wine
- 400g mussels, scrubbed, debearded
- 1/3 cup (80ml) olive oil
- 3 garlic cloves, finely chopped
- 1/4 teaspoon dried chilli flakes
- 400g can Ardmona Rich & Thick Classic Tomatoes

- 2 bay leaves
- 1 thyme sprig
- 6 x 80g whole small fish (such as garfish or whiting), cleaned
- 2 x 80g red mullet fillets, cut into 3 pieces
- 6 green prawns, peeled (tails intact), deveined
- 3 whole small squid (see note), cleaned, tubes and tentacles separated
- 2 tablespoons finely chopped flat-leaf parsley

PREPARATION

Place the wine in a large saucepan and bring to a simmer over medium-high heat Add the mussels, cover, and cook for 2-3 minutes, shaking the pan periodically, until the mussels have opened (discard those that haven't). Put aside after straining and reserving the cooking liquid.

In a wide frypan, heat 2 tablespoons oil over medium heat. Cook, stirring constantly, for 2-3 minutes, until the garlic and chili are softened and fragrant. Toss in the tomatoes, bay leaves, thyme, and mussel liquid that has been set aside. Reduce the heat to low and continue to cook for 3-4 minutes, or until the liquid has slightly reduced. Season the mussels with sea salt and freshly ground pepper in the frypan, then cover and keep warm.

In the meantime, season the remaining seafood. In a wide frypan, heat the remaining 2 tablespoons oil over medium-high heat. Cook whole fish in batches if necessary for 2-3 minutes per side until just done, then remove and set aside. Cook the mullet and prawns separately for 1 minute on each side until cooked through, then set aside. Cook for 30 seconds, stirring continuously, until squid is just done. Pour the hot broth over the mussels and divide the seafood among serving bowls. Serve with a sprinkling of parsley.

SOPA DE ARROZ Y PESCADO (RICE AND SEAFOOD SOUP)

Servings:4

INGREDIENTS

- 1/4 cup (60ml) olive oil
- 1 onion, finely chopped
- 2 garlic cloves, chopped
- 1 fresh chorizo, skinned, chopped
- 1 carrot, chopped
- 1 teaspoon grated orange zest
- 2L fish or chicken stock
- 400g can chopped tomatoes
- 1/3 cup (75g) Calasparra or arborio rice

- 200g skinless salmon fillet, pin-boned, cut into 2cm cubes
- 2 small squid tubes, cleaned, cut into rings
- 12 green prawns, peeled (tails intact), deveined
- 2 tablespoons chopped flat-leaf parsley
- Chopped hard-boiled egg, to garnish

PREPARATION

In a wide saucepan, heat 2 tablespoons oil over medium heat. Combine the onion, garlic, chorizo, carrot, and zest in a large mixing bowl. Cook, stirring regularly, for 10 minutes, or until vegetables are softened and chorizo begins to crisp. Bring the stock, tomato, and rice to a boil, then reduce to a low heat and cook for 15 minutes, or until the rice is al dente.

In a wide frypan, heat the remaining 1 tablespoon oil over high heat. Season the seafood and cook for 1 minute, in batches if necessary, until just opaque. Stir the seafood into the soup and cook for another minute, or until it is thoroughly heated. Pour into bowls and garnish with parsley and an egg, if desired.

SPANISH SEAFOOD SALAD

Servings:4

INGREDIENTS

- 1kg mussels
- 200ml dry white wine
- 1 tablespoon sherry vinegar or red wine vinegar
- 2 tablespoons extra virgin olive oil
- 1 garlic clove, crushed
- 1 green capsicum, finely chopped
- 1 red onion, thinly sliced
- 250g punnet cherry tomatoes, halved
- 1/4 cup coriander sprigs
- 1 tablespoon olive oil
- 1/2 chorizo sausage, thinly sliced into rounds

- 12 scallops (without roe)
- 1 teaspoon smoked paprika (pimenton)
- Saffron rice (optional) and lemon wedges, to serve

PREPARATION

Soak the mussels for one hour in cold water, adjusting the water twice (this helps remove any grit). Drain any mussels with split shells or those that don't close when tapped on the bench sharply. Scrub well and shave any beards.

In a saucepan over medium-high heat, bring the wine to a boil, then reduce to a simmer for 1 minute. Add the mussels, cover, and cook for 2 minutes over medium heat. Remove the mussels that have been opened. Cook for another minute, or until all of the mussels have opened. Remove the liquid from the strainer and set it aside.

Whisk together the vinegar, extra virgin oil, and garlic in a mixing bowl with 2-3 tablespoons of the reserved mussel liquid. Toss in the capsicum, cabbage, tomato, and coriander to mix.

In a wide fry pan, heat the olive oil over medium-high heat. Cook for 1 minute on each hand, or until the chorizo is browned and the scallops are golden. Serve with the salad and saffron rice, if using, after tossing the mussels with the scallops, chorizo, and any pan juices. Serve with a squeeze of lemon and a dusting of paprika.

GRILLED SHELLFISH WITH SHERRY VINAIGRETTE

Servings:8

INGREDIENTS

- 1kg mussels, scrubbed, debearded
- 600g whole small squid, cleaned, tentacles and tubes separated
- 2 tbs olive oil
- 2 tomatoes
- 1kg cooked prawns, peeled, deveined, halved lengthways
- 2 tbs chopped flat-leaf parsley
- 1 red onion, thinly sliced

- 1 green capsicum, finely chopped
- 1 red capsicum, finely chopped
- 4 spring onions, thinly sliced on an angle
- Crusty bread, to serve (optional)
- VINAIGRETTE
- 1/2 cup (125ml) extra virgin olive oil
- 2 tbs sherry vinegar* or red wine vinegar
- 2 garlic cloves, crushed

PREPARATION

Any mussels with split shells or those that won't close after a sharp tap on the bench should be discarded.

Place the mussels and 2 tablespoons water in a big, deep saucepan over high heat, cover, and cook for 2-3 minutes, shaking the pan and giving them a good stir after about 1 minute, removing them as they open. Cook for an additional minute, or until all of the mussels have opened. Remove from the sun, drain, and set aside to cool. Remove mussels from shells and place in a wide mixing bowl until cool enough to treat. Set back, protected.

Meanwhile, split squid tubes into 1cm rings and halve wide tentacle bunches lengthwise. In a wide frypan, heat 1 tablespoon of oil over high heat. Cook, stirring periodically, for about 2 minutes, or until the squid is lightly caramelized and cooked through. Season with freshly ground black pepper and sea salt, then move to a plate to cool. Using the remaining oil and squid, repeat the process.

In the base of each tomato, make a small cross. Blanch for 20 seconds in a large saucepan of boiling water, then cool for 30 seconds in a bowl of ice water. After peeling the tomatoes, quarter them and cut the seeds. Place in the bowl with the mussels after slicing into strips.

Toss the mussels with the prawns, squid, parsley, red onion, capsicum, and spring onion, then gently toss to blend. Cover and chill for at least 15 minutes - the salad can be chilled for up to 2 hours at this stage..

MARISCOS FRITOS (MIXED SEAFOOD) WITH ROMESCO SAUCE

Servings:8

INGREDIENTS

- Sunflower oil, to deep-fry
- 600g small whole squid, cleaned, tentacles and tubes separated
- 400g John Dory fillets, cut in 5cm pieces
- 16 peeled green prawns (tails intact), deveined
- Fine semolina*, to coat
- Lemon wedges, to serve

- Romesco sauce (makes 300ml)
- 2 vine-ripened tomatoes, halved
- 8 hazelnuts
- 1/2 cup (125ml) olive oil
- 1 slice day-old white bread, crust removed, torn
- 4 garlic cloves, chopped
- 1 1/2 tsp dried chilli flakes
- 1 tbs sherry vinegar* or red wine vinegar

PREPARATION

Preheat the oven to 200 degrees Celsius. Place the tomatoes cut-side up in a small roasting pan for the romesco sauce. Season with salt and pepper and bake for 25 minutes, or until tender. Place the nuts on a baking sheet and toast them lightly in the oven for the last 5 minutes of cooking.

Allow tomatoes to cool before peeling. Remove the skins from the nuts by rubbing them in a clean tea towel. In a separate pan, heat 2 tbsp oil over medium heat. Add the bread and cook for 3-4 minutes, rotating once, until golden brown, adding the garlic for the last 2 minutes. Allow to cool slightly before transferring to a food processor. Toss in the tomatoes, nuts, chili, vinegar, remaining 1/3 cup olive oil, 1/2 teaspoon salt, and a pinch of black pepper. Blend until absolutely smooth. (Sauce can be refrigerated for up to two days.)

3.Heat a deep-fryer or a big, deep saucepan half-filled with sunflower oil to 190°C (a cube of bread will turn golden in 30 seconds when the oil is hot enough).

4.Cut squid tubes into 1cm slices, then halve large tentacle clusters lengthwise. All fish should be well-seasoned. Working with four bits at a time, cover completely in semolina and shake off waste.

5.Deep-fry a quarter of the fish and prawns for 1 minute, or until golden crisp. Drain on paper towels for a few minutes before arranging on a platter. Deep-fry one-quarter of the squid for 30 seconds, until golden and crisp, then drain on paper towel before serving. Serve with lemon wedges and romesco sauce right away.

MEXICAN SEAFOOD SOUP

Servings:4

INGREDIENTS

- 1/4 cup (60ml) olive oil
- 500g good-quality seafood marinara mix
- 1 teaspoon smoked paprika (pimenton) (see note)
- 1 onion, finely chopped
- 2 garlic cloves, sliced
- 1 red capsicum, thinly sliced
- 2 jalapeno or long green chillies, seeds removed, finely chopped
- 1/2 teaspoon dried oregano
- 3 teaspoons ground coriander
- 3 teaspoons ground cumin

- 1 teaspoon chilli flakes (optional)
- 2 x 400g cans chopped tomatoes
- 500ml good-quality fish or chicken stock
- 2 corn cobs
- Grated zest & juice of 1 lime
- Sour cream, chopped avocado, coriander leaves & chargrilled tortillas, to serve

PREPARATION

1.In a broad skillet, heat the oil over high heat. Toss the seafood with half of the paprika in a bowl, season, and cook for 2-3 minutes, rotating once, until the seafood is lightly seared and just cooked. Take the seafood out of the pan and set it aside.

2.Add the onion to the pan and cook for 1-2 minutes, stirring occasionally, until softened. Cook, stirring constantly, for 2 minutes, until garlic, capsicum, chili, dried herbs, spices, and the remaining 1/2 teaspoon paprika are soft. Reduce the heat to medium-low and add the tomato and stock. Simmer, stirring regularly, for 12-15 minutes, or until slightly thickened.

3.Cut corn kernels from cobs. Apply the kernels to the soup along with the cooked seafood. To heat up, simmer for 2 minutes. Remove the pan from the heat and add the lime zest and juice. It's that time of year.

4.Serve the soup in four bowls with sour cream, avocado, coriander, and soft tortillas.

SEAFOOD CURRY)

Servings:4

INGREDIENTS

- 2 dried red chillies, soaked in boiling water, drained, chopped
- 3 garlic cloves, chopped
- 1 tablespoon grated fresh turmeric
- 2 tablespoons grated galangal
- 2 lemongrass stems (inner core only), grated
- 2 eschalots, chopped
- Finely grated zest of 1 lime
- 1 tablespoon shrimp paste
- 1/4 cup (65g) grated palm sugar
- 6 kaffir lime leaves, finely shredded

- 400ml coconut milk
- 400g skinless blue-eye fillet, cut into 3-4cm pieces
- 12 green prawns, peeled (tails intact), deveined
- 2 banana leaves
- 1 long red chilli, thinly sliced
- Steamed rice, to serve

PREPARATION

1.In a mortar and pestle or small food processor, pound or whiz the chilli, garlic, turmeric, galangal, lemongrass, eschalot, lime zest, shrimp paste, palm sugar, half the kaffir lime leaves, and 2 teaspoons salt until a fine paste forms.

2.Transfer paste to a medium-sized frypan and cook, stirring continuously, for 3-4 minutes, or until fragrant. Bring the coconut milk to a simmer, reserving 2 tablespoons for serving. Remove from the sun, pour into a cup, and set aside to cool slightly. Toss in the seafood to blend.

SEAFOOD STEW WITH

Servings:4

INGREDIENTS

- 20ml (1 tablespoon) olive oil
- 1 onion, thinly sliced
- 2 garlic cloves, crushed
- 400g kipfler potatoes, peeled, sliced
- 1/2 teaspoon saffron
- 250ml (1 cup) white wine
- 2 tablespoons sun-dried tomato paste
- 400g can crushed tomatoes
- 300ml fish stock

- 1 tablespoon chopped fresh rosemary
- 300g firm white fish fillet, cut into pieces
- 400g black mussels, scrubbed, bearded
- Toasted baguette, to serve

ROUILLE

- 1 roasted red capsicum
- 1 potato, peeled, boiled, diced
- 2 garlic cloves, chopped
- 1 egg yolk
- 125ml (1/2 cup) olive oil

PREPARATION

1.In a large skillet, heat the oil over medium heat. Cook for 1 minute, or until the onion is softened. Simmer for 2 minutes after adding the garlic, potato, saffron, and wine. Cook for 15 minutes after adding the tomato paste, onions, stock, and rosemary.

2. Season the capsicum, potato, garlic, and egg yolk with salt and pepper in a food processor to make the rouille. After combining the ingredients, drizzle in the oil in a thin, steady stream until you have a smooth emulsion.

3.Salt and pepper the stew before adding the fish and mussels. Cook for another 5 minutes, covered. Remove the lid and discard any mussels that haven't opened. Serve with toasted baguette and a dollop of rouille on top of the stew..

SEAFOOD BISQUE

Servings:6

INGREDIENTS

- 1 tablespoon extra virgin olive oil
- 1 tablespoon unsalted butter
- 1 large onion, finely chopped
- 1 medium stalk celery, finely chopped
- 2 tablespoons plain flour
- 1/2 teaspoon cayenne pepper
- 2 teaspoons paprika
- 1 tablespoon tomato paste
- 1L (4 cups) fish stock
- 250ml (1 cup) white wine
- 400g green prawns, shelled, tails on, deveined

- 1kg mixed seafood (such as white fish fillet cut into 2cm cubes, mussels, calamari and scallops)
- 2-3 teaspoons lemon juice
- 100ml thin cream
- 1 tablespoon chopped flat-leaf parsley
- Crusty bread, to serve

PREPARATION

1.In a small saucepan, heat the oil and butter over medium-low heat. Simmer for 2-3 minutes, or until the onion and celery are softened.

2.Add the rice, cayenne pepper, and paprika and cook for 1-2 minutes, stirring constantly. Cook for another minute after adding the tomato paste.

3.Add the fish stock gradually, then reduce heat to low and cook for 5 minutes. Enable to cool slightly before blending in batches and returning to the pan.

4.Bring the white wine and 250ml water to a boil in a saucepan over medium-low heat. Cover and cook for 5 minutes with the prawns and seafood. Using a strainer, separate the liquid from the seafood. (Be sure to throw away any mussels that haven't opened.)

5.Reheat the soup gently, then whisk in the cooked fish, lemon juice, and cream. To mix, stir all together.

6.Ladle the bisque into bowls and top with chopped flat-leaf parsley and plenty of crusty bread.

TROPICAL SEAFOOD COCKTAIL

Servings:6

INGREDIENTS

- 200ml coconut milk
- 1 tablespoon grated fresh ginger
- 1 lemongrass stem (pale part only), finely chopped
- 1 long red chilli, seeds removed, finely chopped
- 150g thick Greek-style yoghurt
- 2 tablespoons finely chopped mint leaves, plus extra leaves to serve

- Grated zest and juice of 1 lime, plus extra lime wedges to serve
- 300g small cooked prawns, peeled
- 1 small cooked lobster, halved, meat cut into 2cm cubes
- 200g fresh crabmeat
- 1/4 small iceberg lettuce, shredded

PREPARATION

1. In a pan, combine the coconut milk, ginger, lemongrass, and half of the chili. Bring to a boil over medium heat, then reduce to a low heat and continue to cook for 2 minutes, or until the sauce has thickened (it will be quite thick). Allow 30 minutes to infuse before straining into a wide bowl and pressing down on solids. After discarding the solids, combine the yoghurt, mint, lime zest and juice, and the remaining chilli in a mixing bowl.

2.Toss the prawns, lobster, and crabmeat in the coconut dressing until completely coated. To serve, split the lettuce into 6 chilled serving glasses, top with the seafood mixture, and garnish with extra mint and lime wedges.

BARBECUED SEAFOOD WITH TRUFFLED MASH

Servings:4

INGREDIENTS

- 1/4 cup (60ml) olive oil
- 3 garlic cloves, crushed
- 2 tablespoons chopped flat-leaf parsley
- Grated zest and juice of 1 lemon, plus lemon wedges to serve
- 4 scampi (see note), halved lengthways, cleaned
- 8 large green prawns, peeled (heads and tails intact), deveined
- 8 large scallops without roe

- 1-2 teaspoons truffle salt (see note) (optional)
- Dressed watercress sprigs, to serve

TRUFFLED MASH

- 500g pontiac or desiree potatoes, peeled
- 80g unsalted butter
- 50ml thickened cream
- 1 tablespoon truffle oil (see note), plus extra to drizzle

PREPARATION

1In a big mixing bowl, combine the olive oil, garlic, parsley, and lemon zest and juice. Turn the scampi, prawns, and scallops in the mixture to coat them, then cover and refrigerate as you make the truffled mash.

2.To make the mash, steam or boil potatoes until tender in salted water for 8-10 minutes. Drain and mash until smooth with a potato ricer or a fork. Stir in the butter, milk, and truffle oil, then season with sea salt and freshly ground black pepper to taste. Keep warm by covering.

3.Heat a chargrill pan or a barbecue to medium-high. Cook the prawns and scampi for 2 minutes on each side, in batches if necessary, until cooked through. Add the scallops for the last minute of cooking, turning after 30 seconds, until golden on the outside but still translucent on the inside.

4.To serve, divide the truffled mash between plates and drizzle with additional truffle oil. Serve with watercress leaves and lemon wedges, as well as truffle salt if desired, on top of the prawns, scampi, and scallops.

SEAFOOD TEMPURA

Servings:16

INGREDIENTS

- 500g cleaned squid (hoods and tentacles)
- 40 green tiger prawns
- 500g skinned John Dory fillet
- Sunflower or canola oil, to deep-fry

SWEET CHILLI AND FIVE-SPICE DIPPING SAUCE

- 300ml Thai sweet chilli sauce
- 2 tbs light soy sauce
- 1/2 tsp five-spice powder
- TEMPURA BATTER
- 1 1/2 cups (225g) plain flour

- 1 1/2 cups (225g) cornflour
- 500-600ml ice-cold soda water (from a new bottle)

PREPARATION

1.To make the dipping sauce, combine all of the ingredients in a small bowl with 1/4 cup (60ml) cold water. Delete from the equation.

2.Split the tentacles into pairs and cut the squid hoods into 1cm thick rings. Remove the heads and peel the prawns, leaving the tails behind. Cut the fish into thick strips about the size of your index finger by cutting it diagonally across..

MEDITERRANEAN SEAFOOD TARTS WITH AIOLI

Servings:6

INGREDIENTS

- 1/4 cup (60ml) olive oil, plus extra to brush
- 2 x 120g skinless salmon fillets
- 12 scallops with roe
- 12 cooked prawns, peeled (tails intact)
- 1 1/2 tablespoons lemon juice
- 1 tablespoon chopped dill, plus sprigs to serve
- Fennel and flat-leaf parsley salad dressed with olive oil and lemon juice, to serve
- PASTRY

- 2 cups (300g) plain flour
- 150g chilled unsalted butter, chopped
- 1/2 teaspoon cayenne pepper
- 2 egg yolks

AIOLI

- 1 cup (250ml) canola oil
- 50ml lemon-infused extra virgin olive oil
- 4 garlic cloves
- 2 tablespoons lemon juice
- 3 egg yolks

PREPARATION

1.In a food processor, pulse flour, butter, cayenne pepper, and a pinch of salt until the mixture resembles fine breadcrumbs. Pulse in the egg yolks and 2 tablespoons chilled water until the mixture forms a smooth ball. Refrigerate for 30 minutes after wrapping in plastic wrap.

2.Preheat the oven to 190 degrees Celsius. On a lightly floured surface, roll out the pastry to a thickness of 3-5mm. To line six 10cm loose-bottomed tart pans, cut six 12cm circles. Line tart shells with baking paper and pastry weights or uncooked rice and place pans on a large baking tray. Remove the paper and weights or rice after 10 minutes of blind baking. Bake for another 3 minutes, or until the pastry is golden and crisp. Allow to cool before removing the shells from the pans.

3.In the meantime, make the aioli by mixing the oils in a jug. In a food processor, mix the garlic, juice, and yolks with a pinch of salt, then process until smooth. While the engine is working, slowly drizzle in the oil until you have a thick mayonnaise. Season to taste, then cover and keep refrigerated until ready to use (up to 4 days).

4.Heat the extra oil in a chargrill pan or a heavy-bottomed frypan over high heat. Cook salmon for 1-2 minutes on each side until just cooked when the pan is hot. Delete from the equation. Scallops should be cooked for 30 seconds on each side, or until just opaque. Break the salmon into chunks and combine with the scallops and prawns in a big mixing bowl. Season with salt and pepper, then toss the seafood gently with the oil, lemon juice, and dill.

5.To serve, spread some aioli on the tart shells, top with the seafood, and finish with a sprig of dill. Serve with a fennel salad.

GRILLED SEAFOOD WITH ROAST VEGETABLE SAUCE

Servings:4

INGREDIENTS

- 500g baby bottle squid, cleaned
- 8 scampi, halved
- 1kg large prawns, head removed (shell and tail left intact), halved lengthways, deveined
- 1/2 cup (125ml) olive oil, plus 2 tbs to dress rocket
- 3 garlic cloves, crushed handful of basil leaves
- 1/3 cup (80ml) lemon juice
- 100g wild rocket leaves

- 1 tbs sherry vinegar
- ROAST VEGETABLE SAUCE
- 2 red capsicums (500g total)
- 1 eggplant
- 2 garlic cloves, chopped
- 6 anchovy fillets, chopped
- 1 tbs salted capers, rinsed
- 1/2 cup (125ml) extra virgin olive oil

PREPARATION

1.Reserve squid tentacles after cutting them off. Open up the tubes and gently score one hand. Combine all of the squid, scampi, and prawns in a dish. Season with salt and pepper, then toss in the seafood with the oil, garlic, basil, and lemon juice. When you're making the sauce, marinate the meat in the fridge.

2.Preheat a lightly oiled barbecue to medium-high heat for the sauce. Capsicums and eggplant should be cooked until the skins are charred and the flesh is softened. Enable to cool in a bowl before covering with plastic wrap. Remove the seeds from the capsicums and mix the flesh in a blender (reserving any juices).

3.Halve the eggplant, scoop out the flesh, and mix with the garlic, anchovies, and capers in a blender. To make a smooth sauce, blend to a puree, then add oil while the motor is still working. (If the sauce is too thick, thin it out with some of the reserved capsicum juice.)

4.Drizzle extra oil and vinegar over the rocket, season, and arrange on plates. Grill the seafood until it is just finished, then put it on the rocket leaves and serve with a side of sauce.

SEAFOOD ICE BOWL

S

Servings:8

INGREDIENTS

- 50 seashells (optional), to decorate
- 36 ice cubes
- 250g each of clams and pipis
- 1 small red onion, finely chopped
- 2 garlic cloves, crushed
- 4 tablespoons chopped fresh chives
- 80ml (1/3 cup) red wine vinegar
- 160ml (8 tablespoons) extra virgin olive oil
- 1 cooked lobster
- 2 cooked blue swimmer crabs
- 20 cooked prawns

- 2 dozen oysters, freshly shucked
- LEMON MAYONNAISE
- 2 cups good-quality mayonnaise
- 150ml creme fraiche
- 1 lemon, zested
- 2 lemons, juiced

PREPARATION

1. You'll need two plastic bowls to make the ice bowl: one with a 3-litre capacity and the other slightly smaller. Fill the larger bowl halfway with ice and shells. Place the smaller bowl on top of the ice and press it down. Use tins to weigh down the top tub.

2.Place in freezer and fill bottom bowl halfway with cold water. Freeze for at least 24 hours.

3.In a bath, mix the clams and pipis with 125ml water and 125ml wine. Cook for 1-2 minutes, covered, over high heat. Liquid and clams or pipis that haven't opened should be discarded. Allow time for cooling.

4.Pour 300ml hot water into the top bowl and set aside for one minute before draining. Remove the outer tub.

5.In a large mixing bowl, season onion, garlic, chives, vinegar, and oil.

6.To make the lemon mayonnaise, whisk together all of the ingredients in a mixing bowl. Season to taste. Toss large seafood with dressing and cut into bite-size pieces. Serve with mayonnaise and a pile of fish in an ice tray.

SAFFRON RICE WITH SEAFOOD (ARROZ AZAFRAN

Servings:4

INGREDIENTS

- 250g medium green prawns
- 1 bay leaf
- 750g mussels, cleaned, de-bearded
- 250ml (1 cup) Spanish white wine
- 1 teaspoon Spanish saffron threads
- 40ml (2 tablespoons) Spanish olive oil
- 2 onion, finely chopped
- 2 garlic cloves, crushed
- 1 red capsicum, de-seeded, chopped

- 300g Calasparra rice
- 750g squid, cleaned, cut into rings
- 1 tablespoon chopped mixed herbs (such as thyme, oregano, parsley)

PREPARATION

1. Shell the prawns and put the heads in a saucepan to make the stock; set aside the meat. Bring to a boil with 750ml (3 cups) water and a bay leaf. Reduce to a low heat and continue to cook for 10 minutes, then strain and set aside the stock. Solids should be discarded.

2.In a saucepan, mix the mussels and wine, cover, and cook over medium heat for about 15 minutes, checking every couple of minutes and removing mussels as they open. (Any mussels that haven't opened should be discarded.) Remove three-quarters of the mussels from their shells, tossing the shells and liquid away. (Save the rest of the mussels in their shells to use as a garnish.)

3.In a heavy-bottomed pan, heat the oil over medium heat. Dry-roast the saffron until fragrant. Cover and set aside to steep the reserved stock.

4.In a medium saucepan, heat the olive oil. Sauté the onion, garlic, and capsicum for 3-4 minutes, or until the onion softens. Reduce heat to minimum, cover, and cook for 20 minutes with the rice and saffron stock. Check for doneness and cook for a few minutes longer if possible, until the rice is tender and most of the liquid has been absorbed. Cook for 5 minutes, or until the squid, reserved prawns, and herbs are just finished. Add the mussels and serve immediately, garnished with the mussels in their shells that were set aside.

SEAFOOD STEW

Servings:8

INGREDIENTS

- 1/4 cup (60ml) olive oil
- 1 onion, thinly sliced
- 1 fennel bulb, thinly sliced
- 2 carrots, peeled, thinly sliced
- 2 garlic cloves, crushed
- 1/2 teaspoon saffron threads
- 1 teaspoon fennel seeds
- 1 long red chilli, seeds removed, finely chopped
- 1L (4 cups) fish stock
- 800g can crushed tomatoes
- 2 bay leaves

- 1 cup (250ml) white wine
- 1kg mussels, de-bearded
- 6 small calamari (including tentacles), cleaned, cut into rings
- 16 green prawns, peeled (tails intact), deveined
- 500g firm white fish (such as blue-eye cod), skin removed, cut into 2cm pieces
- 2 cooked blue swimmer crabs, chopped
- Gremolata, to serve

PREPARATION

In a big frypan, heat 2 tablespoons olive oil. Toss in the onion, fennel, and carrots. Cook for 2-3 minutes over low heat, or until softened. Cook for another minute after adding the garlic, saffron strings, fennel seeds, and chilli. Enable the fish stock, tomatoes, and bay leaves to simmer for 20 minutes over low heat (this dish can be prepared up to this stage well in advance, if desired). Place wine in a saucepan just before serving the stew, add mussels, and cook, covered, over high heat until mussels open (discard any that do not open). Cooking wine should be strained into the stew foundation, but the mussels should be preserved.

2.Preheat the pan in which the mussels were fried. Heat the remaining oil, then quickly add the calamari and cook for 1-2 minutes. Apply to the stew.

3.Cook the prawns and fish in the pan for 1-2 minutes on either side, or until just done. Then add the crab and mussels that were set aside to the stew. Simmer, stirring occasionally, for 2-3 minutes over low heat.

4. Season generously with salt and black pepper. Serve in large bowls of gremolata on top.

THAI SEAFOOD RISOTTO

Servings:4

INGREDIENTS

- 3 tablespoons light olive oil
- 1 medium onion, finely chopped
- 2 garlic cloves, crushed
- 2 tablespoons Thai red curry paste
- 300g arborio rice
- 300ml fish or vegetable stock
- 300ml coconut milk
- 4 fresh kaffir lime leaves, finely shredded
- 1 lemon grass stalk, finely chopped
- 1 (about 200g) medium squid, cleaned, cut into rings

- 200g green prawns, peeled, with tails on
- 150g cleaned scallops
- 1 tablespoon seasoned flour

PREPARATION

1. Preheat the oven to 180 degrees Celsius.

2.In a pan, heat 1 tablespoon of oil and add the onion. Cook for 1 minute over medium heat, or until softened. Combine the garlic and curry paste in a mixing dish. To release the flavors, cook for 1 minute. Cook for 1-2 minutes, stirring constantly. Combine the stock, coconut milk, and half of the lime leaves in a mixing bowl. Salt and pepper to taste. Over high flame, bring to a boil. Remove the pan from the heat and set it aside.

3.In a greased ovenproof bowl, carefully pour the mixture, cover with aluminum foil, and bake for 15 minutes. Remove from the oven and stir thoroughly. Add 1/2 cup water or stock if the mixture is too dry. Cover and bake for an additional 10 minutes. Stir in half of the seafood, cover, and bake for another 10 minutes, or until the seafood is completely cooked.

4.Toss the remaining seafood in the seasoned flour in the meantime.

5.In a clean frying pan, heat the remaining oil, then add the seafood and cook over high heat until crisp.

6.Be sure to give the risotto a good stir. Garnish with the remaining lime leaves and pan-fried seafood.

SEAFOOD CURRY

Servings:4

INGREDIENTS

- 2 tablespoons vegetable oil
- 1 onion, thinly sliced
- 1 garlic clove, crushed
- 2cm piece ginger, grated
- 2 tablespoons mild curry paste
- 1 tablespoon tomato puree
- 500g white fish fillets (such as blue-eye or perch), deboned, cut into 2cm chunks
- 300g green prawns, peeled, tails intact
- 2 x 270ml cans coconut milk
- 1/4 cup (60ml) fish stock or chicken stock

- 1 teaspoon palm or caster sugar
- 2 tablespoons lime juice
- 2 tablespoons chopped coriander leaves, plus whole leaves to garnish
- Steamed brown medium grain rice, to serve
- Lime wedges, to serve

PREPARATION

1.In a heavy-bottomed frypan, heat the oil over medium heat. Cook, stirring constantly, until the onion is softened. Cook for a few seconds after adding the garlic and ginger.

2.Add the curry paste and tomato puree and cook for 1 minute, stirring constantly, until fragrant.

3.Add the seafood to the pan and cover thoroughly. Season with salt and pepper after adding the coconut milk, stock, and sugar. Bring to a boil, then reduce to a low heat and cook for another 10 minutes, or until the seafood is completely cooked. Combine the lime juice and chopped coriander in a mixing bowl. Garnish with coriander leaves and a lime wedge and serve with steamed rice.

SEAFOOD IN CHARDONNAY JELLY

Servings:4

INGREDIENTS

- 3 gelatine leaves*
- 200ml chardonnay
- 1 1/2 tablespoons fish sauce
- 200g cooked small school prawns, peeled, tails intact
- 120g cooked blue swimmer crabmeat
- 100g smoked salmon, cut into thin strips
- Juice of 1/2 lemon
- 1 tablespoon chopped dill

- Melba toasts, to serve

PREPARATION

1. Chill 4 big martini glasses (or similar).

2.Soften gelatine leaves by soaking them in cold water (about 5 minutes).

3.Reduce the wine in a pan over high heat by half. Squeeze out the gelatine and put it in the pan. Stir until the sugar is fully dissolved. Put in a measuring jug with the fish sauce and enough cold water to make 600ml of liquid.

4.Toss the seafood with the lemon and dill in a dish. Toss in the seasonings and whisk to mix.

5.In each bottle, layer a small amount of seafood, top with a little wine mixture, and chill for 15 minutes to set. Repeat until the glasses are fully full and set. Melba toasts are a perfect accompaniment..

FRITTO MISTO (FRIED SEAFOOD AND VEGETABLES)

Servings:6

INGREDIENTS

- 250g squid tubes, sliced into rings
- 12 green prawns, peeled, deveined, tails intact
- 400g firm white fish, cut into 2cm pieces
- 100g whitebait
- 2 (about 200g) zucchini, thinly sliced
- 1 bunch thin asparagus, ends trimmed
- 12 sage leaves
- 1 cup (150g) self-raising flour
- 1 tablespoon cornflour

- 1/2 teaspoon bicarbonate of soda
- Sunflower oil, for deep-frying
- Lemon wedges, to serve

PREPARATION

1.To eliminate any excess moisture, put the fish, vegetables, and sage on a paper towel. To make a smooth batter, sift self-raising flour and corn flour into a mixing bowl, add bicarbonate of soda, season with salt and pepper, and slowly whisk in 350ml chilled water.

2.Heat a deep-fryer or a large saucepan to 190°C and half-fill with oil. (Oil is ready when a cube of bread turns golden in 30 seconds.) Working in batches, dip the vegetables, spices, and seafood into the batter and fry until golden, shifting the pieces around to avoid clumping. Remove from the oven, drain on paper towels, and remain warm until all is finished. Serve with lemon wedges and a pinch of sea salt.

MIXED SEAFOOD GRILL WITH TOMATO VINAIGRETTE

Servings:4

INGREDIENTS

- 8 green prawns
- 8 frozen scampi*, thawed
- 500g piece tuna steak
- Light olive oil, to coat
- 1/4 cup flat-leaf parsley leaves
- 1 lemon, quartered, to serve
- DRESSING
- 1 tomato, finely chopped
- 1 garlic clove, crushed

- 1 tablespoon lemon juice
- 1/4 cup (60ml) olive oil

PREPARATION

1. .To make the dressing, whisk together the tomato, garlic, lemon juice, and olive oil until smooth, then season with sea salt and freshly ground black pepper to taste.

2.Devein the prawns by removing the heads and butterflying around the back.

3.Cut the scampi in half lengthwise, remove the vein, and rinse under cold water to clean. Make four tiny steaks out of the tuna. Coat all in olive oil and season with salt and pepper.

4.Preheat a chargrill or barbecue that has been lightly oiled to medium-high heat. When the grill is hot, place the prawns and scampi cut-side down on the grill (in batches if necessary). Cook for 1-2 minutes on one side until well-colored, then flip and cook for 30-60 seconds on the other side or until just cooked through. Cook the tuna on one side for 1-2 minutes, turning halfway through to create criss-cross grill marks. Cook for an additional minute on the other hand.

5. Arrange all of the seafood on a large serving platter in a relaxed manner. Spread the dressing on top and garnish with parsley.

6.Serve with lemon wedges on the side. s.

PREPARATION

BARBECUED SEAFOOD SKEWERS WITH ROMESCO SAUCE

Servings:12

INGREDIENTS

- 12 scallops without roe
- 8 spring onions, each cut into 4 lengths
- 12 green prawns, peeled (tails intact), deveined
- 6 asparagus spears, woody ends trimmed, each cut into 4 lengths, lightly blanched
- Olive oil, to brush
- Small lemon wedges, to serve
- ROMESCO SAUCE

- 1/3 cup (80ml) fruity or low-acid extra virgin olive oil
- 10 hazelnuts
- 10 blanched almonds
- 1 slice white bread, crusts removed
- 5 piquillo pimientos (about 100g)
- 1/4 teaspoon smoked paprika
- Small pinch cayenne pepper
- 4 garlic cloves
- 2 teaspoons sherry vinegar
- 1 ripe tomato, peeled, seeds removed, roughly chopped

PREPARATION

1. To avoid scorching, soak 12 wooden skewers (or trimmed bay leaf twigs for a rustic look) in cold water for 2 hours.

2.In a small saucepan over medium-low heat, heat 2 tablespoons of oil for the romesco sauce. Cook, stirring constantly, for 5 minutes or until golden. Remove the nuts and place them on a crumpled paper towel to drain. Fry the bread in the pan for 2 minutes on either side, or until golden. Allow to cool slightly before blending with the nuts, pimientos, paprika, cayenne pepper, garlic, vinegar, tomato, and remaining oil in a food processor to make a paste. Season to taste.

3. Extract any nerves, membranes, or hard white muscle from scallops by slicing or pulling them out. Rinse thoroughly and rinse with a paper towel. On a

skewer, thread two bits of onion. Thread a prawn onto a skewer by curling the ends together. Thread two pieces of asparagus, then a scallop, onto the thread. To make 12 skewers, repeat with the remaining onion, prawns, asparagus, and scallops.

CRUMBED FISH BITES

Servings:24

INGREDIENTS

- 500g fish fillets (salmon or ling)
- 1 cup mashed potato, chilled
- 4 spring onions, chopped
- 2 tbs chopped flat leaf parsley
- 1 tbs hot English mustard
- 1 egg yolk
- ⅓ cup plain flour
- 1 egg, whisked
- 1 cup panko breadcrumbs
- Vegetable oil, to fry

- Whole egg mayonnaise and extra parsley, to serve

PREPARATION

1. In a food processor, puree the fish until it forms a paste. Combine potato, onion, parsley, mustard, and egg yolk in a mixing dish. Season with salt and pepper to taste.

2.Make balls out of tablespoonfuls of the fish mixture. Using flour, egg, and breadcrumbs, coat each fish ball. Place on a serving tray.

3.In a saucepan, heat the oil over medium-high heat. In batches, gently drop the balls into the oil and cook for 1-2 minutes, or until golden. Serve with mayonnaise and parsley on top..

JAMIE OLIVER'S FISH AND CHEAT'S CHIPS WITH

Servings:4

INGREDIENTS

- 1/3 cup (50g) plain flour
- 2 eggs, lightly beaten
- 3 cups (210g) fresh breadcrumbs
- 1 tsp dried chilli flakes
- 4 skinless flounder fillets (order from your fishmonger), cut into 4cm-wide strips
- Sunflower oil, to shallow-fry Cress or micro herbs, to serve

CHEAT'S CHIPS

- 1kg sebago potatoes, scrubbed (unpeeled), cut into 1cm-thick chips
- 3 rosemary sprigs, leaves picked
- 1/4 cup (60ml) olive oil
- 2 garlic cloves, thinly sliced
- MUSHY PEAS
- 25g unsalted butter
- 400g fresh peas (or frozen, thawed)
- 1 small bunch tarragon, leaves finely chopped
- Juice of 1/2 lemon, plus lemon wedges to serve

PREPARATION

1. Preheat the oven to 200 degrees Celsius. Par-boil the potatoes for 3-4 minutes in a saucepan of boiling salted water for the chips. Set aside to cool and dry after draining.

2.Toss the chips with rosemary, oil, and a pinch of salt on a baking tray. After 20 minutes in the oven, remove the tray from the oven and stir in the garlic. Bake for another 15-20 minutes, or until golden and crisp.

3.In the meantime, melt butter in a pan over medium heat for mushy peas. Cook, covered, for 10 minutes (3 minutes for frozen) or until soft, adding fresh peas and tarragon as desired. Season with lemon juice. Mash until the mixture is mushy. To keep warm, cover.

4. Divide the rice, egg, and breadcrumbs into three bowls. Season the crumbs with salt and pepper, as well

as the chilli flakes. Fish should be floured first, then dipped in egg, shaking off any excess, and then breadcrumb-coated. Season with salt and pepper, set aside, and repeat with the remaining fish.

CRISPY CRUMBED FISH WITH ROASTED CARROTS AND

Servings:4

INGREDIENTS

- 3 large carrots, cut into large batons
- 1 tsp paprika
- Pinch of cayenne pepper
- 1/4 cup (60ml) extra virgin olive oil
- 3/4 cup (75g) dried breadcrumbs
- 4 x 150g thick skinless white fish fillets (such as blue-eye)
- 50g unsalted butter, melted
- 1/2 bunch watercress, sprigs picked

- 1 orange, peeled, pith removed, segmented
- 1/2 red onion, thinly sliced
- 1/2 cup (60g) pitted black olives, halved
- 1 tbs white wine vinegar
- 1/2 cup (150g) whole-egg mayonnaise
- 1 tbs harissa

PREPARATION

1.Preheat the oven to 220 degrees Celsius and line two baking trays with parchment paper.

2. Season carrots with spices and 1 tablespoon oil. Spread on a baking sheet and bake for 15-20 minutes, or until softened.

3.In the meantime, season the breadcrumbs and spread them out on a tray. Brush the fish with butter and then roll it in the crumbs. Place the fish on the second tray. Bake for another 15 minutes, or until the fish is crisp and cooked through, and the carrots are golden brown.

4.In a mixing bowl, combine the cress, orange, onion, and olives. Season with salt and pepper, then pour the vinegar and remaining 2 tablespoons oil over the salad and toss to blend.

BRAISED FISH WITH CHORIZO, CAPSICUM AND POTATOES

Servings:4

INGREDIENTS

- 2 tbs olive oil
- 1 chorizo, skin removed, finely chopped
- 2 onions, chopped
- 1 red capsicum, roughly chopped
- 1 green capsicum, roughly chopped
- 1 tsp smoked paprika (pimenton)*
- 6 anchovies in oil, roughly chopped
- 500g waxy potatoes, peeled, cut into 2cm chunks

- 400ml dry white wine
- 4 x 150g thick white fish fillets (such as ling)
- Chopped flat-leaf parsley, to serve

PREPARATION

1. In a deep nonstick frypan, heat the oil over medium heat. Cook, stirring occasionally, until chorizo, onion, capsicum, paprika, and anchovies are translucent and chorizo begins to brown, 3-4 minutes.

2.Add the potato to the pan, cover partially with the lid, and cook for 25 minutes, or until the potatoes are almost tender and the vegetables are soft.

3.Add the wine to the pan, bring to a boil, then reduce to medium-low heat and continue to cook for 2-3 minutes, or until slightly reduced. Add the fish, cover, and cook for 6-8 minutes, or until the fish is just done. Serve immediately with a parsley garnish, or switch to a serving dish before serving.

BAKED FISH WITH CAPERS, POTATO AND LEMON

Servings:4

INGREDIENTS

- 8 small chat potatoes, skin on, very thinly sliced (a mandoline or vegetable peeler is ideal)
- 1/4 cup (60ml) extra virgin olive oil
- 4 x 200g skinless firm white fish fillets (such as snapper)
- 1/2 lemon, thinly sliced
- 1 tbs baby salted capers, rinsed, drained
- Handful of soft herbs (such as coriander, flat-leaf parsley, dill, tarragon, chervil or fennel), chopped

PREPARATION

1.Preheat the oven to 200°C and a baking tray to 180°C. Lay out four large sheets of baking paper and four large sheets of foil.

2.Divide the potato between the sheets of paper, adding two layers in the middle of each sheet. Drizzle with half of the olive oil and season with salt and pepper. Top with a fish fillet and a lemon slice, then capers, mixed herbs, and sea salt. Drizzle the remaining 112 tbsp olive oil over everything. Cover the fish in plastic wrap, tucking the ends under to form a parcel, and protect with foil. Bake for 20-30 minutes, until the potato is tender, on the preheated baking sheet.

SMOKED OCEAN TROUT WITH BANANA BLOSSOM AND

Servings:4

INGREDIENTS

- 1/3 cup coconut oil
- 2 x 200g fillets hot-smoked ocean trout
- 4 banana blossom leaves, thinly sliced
- 1/2 cup Thai basil leaves
- 1/2 cup coriander leaves
- 2 tbs thinly sliced garlic, fried, cooled
- 1 tbs fried Asian shallots

- 1 red chilli, seeds removed, shredded
- 2 dried long red chillies, crumbled
- 2 kaffir lime leaves, finely shredded
- Lime wedges, to serve
- SWEET FISH SAUCE
- 250g palm sugar, grated
- 1/2 red onion, sliced
- 1 lemongrass stalk, bruised
- 4 kaffir lime leaves
- 3cm piece of galangal or ginger, sliced
- 4 coriander roots, trimmed
- 2 tbs each fish sauce and tamarind paste

PREPARATION

1. Heat the sugar and 2 tbsp water in a saucepan over medium heat, stirring constantly, until the sugar dissolves. Bring to a boil with the onion, lemongrass, kaffir lime leaves, galangal, and coriander.

2.Reduce to medium-low heat and continue to cook for 5-6 minutes, or until lightly caramelized. Combine the fish sauce and tamarind in a mixing bowl. Remove from the sun, strain, and set aside to cool.

3.In a medium-high-heat frypan, heat the oil and fry the trout for 1-2 minutes on each side, or until warmed through. Remove the meat, rinse it on a paper towel, and cut it into large chunks.

4.Assemble the trout and the rest of the ingredients on plates, then drizzle with the sauce.

SWORDFISH INVOLTINI WITH CAPERS, TOMATOES

Servings:4

INGREDIENTS

- 1 thick slice of bread, such as sourdough or ciabatta, crust removed, torn
- 1 tbs marjoram leaves
- 2 x 180g swordfish fillets, skin removed
- 1 tbs extra virgin olive oil, plus extra to drizzle
- 1 small garlic clove, thinly sliced
- Small pinch of dried chilli flakes
- 1 1/2 tbs pine nuts (optional)
- 250g vine-ripened cherry tomatoes, halved

- 1 tbs salted capers, rinsed
- 1/3 cup (55g) kalamata olives, pitted
- 100ml dry white wine (such as pinot grigio)
- Small handful each of flat-leaf parsley and fennel fronds (optional), chopped

PREPARATION

1. Heat the sugar and 2 tbsp water in a saucepan over medium heat, stirring constantly, until the sugar dissolves. Bring to a boil with the onion, lemongrass, kaffir lime leaves, galangal, and coriander.

2.Reduce to medium-low heat and continue to cook for 5-6 minutes, or until lightly caramelized. Combine the fish sauce and tamarind in a mixing bowl. Remove from the sun, strain, and set aside to cool.

3.In a medium-high-heat frypan, heat the oil and fry the trout for 1-2 minutes on each side, or until warmed through. Remove the meat, rinse it on a paper towel, and cut it into large chunks.

4.Assemble the trout and the rest of the ingredients on plates, then drizzle with the sauce.

SEARED BEEF WITH CARAMEL FISH SAUCE AND LIME SLAW

Servings:4

INGREDIENTS

- 250g palm sugar, grated
- 1/4 cup (60ml) best-quality fish sauce
- 1/4 cup (60ml) lime juice
- 1kg prime grass-fed fillet of beef
- 6 long red chillies, seeds removed, thinly sliced
- RAW SLAW
- 2 cups each thinly sliced white
- cabbage and iceberg lettuce, (a mandoline is ideal)

- Juice of 3 plump limes

PREPARATION

1.Place the sugar and 1 cup (250ml) water in a saucepan over medium heat, stirring until sugar dissolves. Bring to the boil and simmer for 12-15 minutes, until the mixture has thickened and become a light caramel colour. Remove from the heat, then add the fish sauce and lime juice, gently swirling to combine. Set the fish sauce caramel aside.

2.Preheat the barbecue hotplate to full heat.

3.For the raw slaw, combine the cabbage and lettuce in a large bowl, season with salt and pepper, then dress generously with the lime juice. Set aside.

4.Use your hands to rub 1 tsp sea salt all over the beef. Sear for 1-2 minutes each side until brown all over (be sure to always apply the meat to a spot on the grill that has not had its heat dissipated by cooking). Remove from heat, rest for 5 minutes, then slice - it will be very rare in the middle.

5.Place the slaw on a serving platter, then top with the sliced beef. Garnish with chilli, then serve drizzled with the caramel.

KINGFISH CARPACCIO WITH GREEN CHILLI PASTE

Servings:4

INGREDIENTS

- 600g sashimi-grade kingfish*
- 4 long green chillies, seeds removed, finely chopped
- 1/2 cup coriander leaves
- Juice of 4 limes
- 1/3 cup (80ml) olive oil
- 1/3 cup (80ml) Japanese soy sauce
- Micro herbs or baby salad leaves, to serve

PREPARATION

1. Chill the fish slices, which should be 5mm thick, until ready to eat.

2.Pulse the chilli and coriander until a paste develops in the bowl of a small food processor. Mix in the lime juice and just enough oil to make it sticky (you want to end up with a loose, smooth paste).

3.Place the fish on a serving platter and drizzle with soy sauce. Garnish with micro herbs after sprinkling the fish with chilli paste.

CHERMOULA KINGFISH WITH MOROCCAN BEANS

Servings:4

INGREDIENTS

- 4 x 180g skinless kingfish fillets
- 2 tablespoons olive oil
- 1 onion, finely chopped
- 2 garlic cloves, crushed
- 720g can mixed beans, rinsed, drained
- 1/4 cup sliced roasted capsicum
- 1/2 cup (125ml) chicken stock
- 1/2 cup coriander leaves
- CHERMOULA

- 2 teaspoons sweet paprika
- 1 teaspoon finely grated ginger
- 1 teaspoon dried chilli flakes
- 1 teaspoon ground cumin
- 1 teaspoon ground coriander
- 1 teaspoon ground white pepper
- 1/2 teaspoon ground cardamom
- 1/2 teaspoon ground cinnamon
- 1/2 teaspoon ground all spice
- 2 tablespoons lemon juice
- 1/4 cup (60ml) olive oil

PREPARATION

1. In a large mixing bowl, combine all of the ingredients for the chermoula.

2.Toss the kingfish in the chermoula to evenly coat it. Organize

3.In a wide saucepan, heat 1 tablespoon oil and add the onion. Cook for 2-3 minutes, stirring occasionally, until softened, then add the garlic and cook for an additional 2 minutes, or until fragrant. Remove the pan from the sun.

4.In a food processor, whiz 1/2 cup mixed beans until smooth. Combine the bean puree, capsicum, chicken stock, and the remaining beans in a saucepan. Cook for another 2-3 minutes, or until thoroughly warmed. Keep yourself wet.

5.In a medium-sized frypan, heat the remaining 1 tablespoon oil. Cook the kingfish fillets for 2-3 minutes on each hand, or until they are just finished.

6.Garnish with coriander and feed the kingfish with the Moroccan bean mixture.

CHINESE STEAMED FISH WITH GINGER

Servings:4

INGREDIENTS

- 4 x 200g skinless blue-eye fillets
- 5cm piece ginger, thinly sliced
- 100ml chicken stock
- 1/4 cup (60ml) Chinese rice wine (shaohsing)
- 4 baby bok choy, quartered
- 2 tablespoons light soy sauce
- 1 teaspoon caster sugar
- 1/2 teaspoon sesame oil
- 2 tablespoons peanut oil

- 4 spring onions, thinly sliced
- Coriander and steamed rice, to serve

PREPARATION

1. Place the fish in a bamboo steamer on a tray. Pour in the stock and rice wine after scattering the ginger. Cover and steam for 5 minutes over a pan of simmering water, then add bok choy, cover, and steam for 2 minutes more, or until fish is cooked.

2.In the meantime, warm the soy, sugar, sesame, and peanut oil in a pan over medium heat for 2 minutes.

3.Toss the fish and bok choy with the dressing, coriander, and rice..

SMOKY FISH AND PRAWN PIE

S

Servings:4

INGREDIENTS

- 750g smoked cod fillets
- 2 1/2 cups (625ml) milk
- 1 small onion, roughly chopped
- 1 bay leaf
- 1/4 cup chopped tarragon leaves
- 75g unsalted butter, chopped
- 1/3 cup (50g) plain flour
- 1kg potatoes, cut into 4cm pieces
- 100g smoked cheddar, grated
- 350g green prawn meat

PREPARATION

1Preheat the oven to 200 degrees Celsius. In a deep frypan over medium heat, combine the fish, milk, onion, bay leaf, and 1 tablespoon tarragon. Season with salt and pepper and bring to a boil, then reduce to low heat and simmer for 5 minutes, or until the flavors have infused. Remove the fish from the pan and set it aside. Fill a jug halfway with milk and strain it.

2.In a saucepan over medium heat, melt 50g butter. Cook, stirring constantly, for 2-3 minutes, or until pale golden. Whisk in the milk until creamy, then cook for 2 minutes, stirring constantly, until slightly thickened. Season with the remaining 2 teaspoons tarragon.

3.In the meantime, bring a pot of salted water to a boil and cook the potato for 15 minutes, or until tender. Drain the potato, then return it to the pan and cook for 30 seconds to remove any remaining liquid. Season with salt and pepper after mashing the potato with 75g cheese and the remaining 25g butter.

4.Flake the fish, discarding the meat, and combine with the prawns and sauce in a 2L (8-cup) ovenproof bowl, stirring to combine. Spread the mashed potato on top, making sure it completely covers the filling. Sprinkle the remaining 25g of cheese on top and bake for 30-35 minutes, or until golden and bubbling.

5.Set aside for 5 minutes to cool before serving.

CHARGRILLED SWORDFISH WITH GRAPE, ALMOND & BARLEY SALAD

Servings:4

INGREDIENTS

- 1 1/4 cups (280g) pearl barley, rinsed
- Finely grated zest and juice of 1/2 lemon
- 2 tsp dried Italian herbs
- 100ml olive oil
- 4 x 220g swordfish fillets
- 1 1/2 tbs red wine vinegar
- 225g red seedless grapes, halved
- 1/2 cup (80g) roasted almonds, chopped

- 1/3 cup (60g) currants, soaked in warm water for 10 minutes, drained
- 1 bunch flat-leaf parsley, leaves picked
- 2 celery stalks, chopped

PREPARATION

1. In a saucepan of boiling salted water, cook barley for 25-30 minutes, or until tender. Drain the water and set it aside to cool.

2.In a separate cup, mix lemon zest, 1 teaspoon Italian herbs, and 2 tablespoons oil. Season with salt and pepper, then add the swordfish and toss to cover. Set aside for 15 minutes to marinate.

3.To make the dressing, combine the vinegar, lemon juice, and the remaining 1/4 cup (60ml) oil in a mixing bowl, season with salt and pepper, and set aside.

4.Preheat a chargrill pan or a barbecue to high heat. Swordfish should be cooked for 3 minutes on each side or until just finished. Rest for 5 minutes, loosely covered with foil.

5.Combine the barley, grapes, almonds, currants, parsley, celery, and the remaining 1 tablespoon Italian herbs in a mixing bowl. Drizzle the dressing over the salad and toss to mix.

6.Serve the salad with swordfish on top.

QUICK FILO FISH PIE

S

Servings:4

INGREDIENTS

- 1 cup (250ml) milk
- 2 eggs, lightly beaten
- 1 tablespoon dill, chopped
- 1/2 cup (140g) thick Greek-style yoghurt
- 1/2 teaspoon smoked paprika (pimenton)
- 16 green prawns, peeled, deveined
- 2 x 150g hot-smoked salmon fillets, flaked
- 1 cup (120g) frozen peas, thawed
- 1 baby fennel bulb, very finely chopped
- 8 sheets filo pastry
- 100g unsalted butter, melted, cooled slightly

- Lemon wedges, to serve

PREPARATION

1. Preheat the oven to 180 degrees Celsius.

2.In a mixing bowl, whisk together the milk, eggs, dill, yoghurt, and paprika. Pour the milk mixture over the prawns, salmon, peas, and fennel in four 350ml ovenproof bowls. On a clean work surface, lay out two sheets of filo. Brush with butter, then scrunch up and put on top of pie filling gently. Rep with the rest of the filo and pies.

3.Bake for 30 minutes, or until the pastry is golden and crisp and the prawns are cooked through. Enable to cool slightly. Lemon wedges can be served with the pies.

CACCIUCCO CON POLENTA (TUSCAN FISH STEW WITH

Servings:4

INGREDIENTS

- 1/4 cup (60ml) extra virgin olive oil
- 2 garlic cloves, finely chopped
- 2 tbs finely chopped flat-leaf parsley leaves, plus extra leaves to serve
- 1/4 cup (60ml) white wine
- 2 x 400g cans chopped tomatoes
- 1.5L (6 cups) fish stock
- 300g skinless ling or barramundi fillet, pin-boned, cut into 3cm pieces

- 12 green prawns, peeled (tails intact), deveined
- 8 scallops, roe removed
- 8 mussels, debearded, scrubbed
- 8 clams, rinsed
- 11/2 cups (250g) instant polenta

PREPARATION

1.In a large saucepan with a lid, heat the oil over medium-high heat. Cook, stirring constantly, for 1-2 minutes, until garlic and parsley are fragrant. Pour in the wine and continue to cook for another 2-3 minutes, or until the wine has fully evaporated. Bring to a boil with the chopped tomatoes and fish stock, then reduce to medium-low and cook for 20-30 minutes, until reduced and slightly thickened. Cook for 1 minute after adding the fish and prawns, then cover and cook for another 1-2 minutes, shaking the pot once or twice, until the mussels and clams have opened and the seafood is cooked through. Remove the pan from the sun.

2.In the meantime, cook the polenta according to the package directions. It's that time of year.

3.Divide the polenta into four cups, ladle over the stew, and cover with parsley leaves.

KINGFISH AND PRAWN CEVICHE

Servings:6

INGREDIENTS

- 1 red onion, thinly sliced
- 200g peeled green prawns, deveined
- 200g skinless sashimi-grade kingfish fillets (see note), pin-boned, cut into 1cm pieces
- 1 garlic clove, crushed
- 1 long green chilli, seeds removed, finely chopped
- 2 tbs finely chopped coriander
- 1 cup (250ml) lime juice (from about 7 limes), plus wedges to serve
- 2 tbs extra virgin olive oil

- Rye bread croutons, to serve

PREPARATION

1. Soak the onion for 10 minutes in a tub of cold water. Drain the water and set it aside.

2.In the meantime, over medium-low heat, bring a small saucepan of water to a simmer. Prepare the prawns by blanching them.

Combine the kingfish, chopped prawns, garlic, chili, and coriander in a ceramic or glass dish. Season, then stir in 5 ice cubes and enough lime juice to almost cover the mixture. Apply one-third of the onion and stir to combine; after a few moments, the lime juice should turn a whitish hue. Season the ceviche with salt and pepper to taste.

4.Stir in the oil after removing the ice cubes. Serve with croutons and lime wedges and garnished with the remaining onion.

KERALAN FISH CURRY

Servings:4

INGREDIENTS

- 2 tablespoons sunflower oil
- 2 teaspoons panch phoran (Indian spice mix) (see note)
- 20 fresh curry leaves (see note)
- 2 onions, thinly sliced
- 2 teaspoons ground turmeric
- 1 cinnamon quill
- 2 long red chillies, seeds removed, finely chopped
- 4cm piece ginger, finely grated
- 2 teaspoons ground cumin

- 1kg firm white fish fillets (such as ling) cut into 4cm cubes
- 400ml coconut milk
- 400g can chopped tomatoes
- 2 teaspoons tamarind puree (see note)
- 1 teaspoon caster sugar
- Steamed basmati rice, coriander leaves and lime wedges, to serve

PREPARATION

1.In a broad frypan, heat the sunflower oil over medium heat. Cook, stirring continuously, for 1-2 minutes, until the panch phoran and curry leaves are fragrant. Cook, stirring occasionally, for 5-6 minutes, or until the onion is soft, then add the turmeric, cinnamon, chili, ginger, and cumin, and cook, stirring constantly, for 1 minute, or until fragrant.

2.Toss in the fish, gently stirring to cover it in the sauce, then add the coconut milk, chopped tomato, and 1/2 cup (125ml) water. Cook for 10-15 minutes, or until the fish is cooked through. Season with sea salt and freshly ground pepper after stirring in the tamarind puree and caster sugar.

3.Distribute the fish curry among steamed rice bowls. Serve with lime wedges and coriander leaves on top.

CRISPY FISH TACOS WITH MANGO SALSA

Servings:10

INGREDIENTS

- 1/3 cup (50g) plain flour
- 1 teaspoon smoked paprika (pimenton)
- 1 teaspoon ground cumin
- 2 eggs, lightly beaten
- 3 cups (150g) panko breadcrumbs (see notes)
- 500g flathead fillets, cut into 20 strips
- Sunflower oil, to deep-fry
- 10 mini flour tortillas
- 1/4 iceberg lettuce, shredded

- 200g sour cream
- Hot sauce (such as Tabasco) or finely chopped long red chilli, to serve

MANGO SALSA

- 1 mango, chopped
- 1 avocado, chopped
- 1/2 red onion, finely chopped
- 2 tablespoons chopped coriander, plus extra leaves to serve
- Juice of 1 lime, plus wedges to serve

PREPARATION

1.Season flour and spices in a mixing bowl. Separate the egg and the breadcrumbs into two cups. The fish should be floured first, then dipped in the egg, and then thoroughly coated in breadcrumbs. Allow 15 minutes for chilling.

2.To make the mango salsa, combine all of the ingredients in a mixing bowl, season with salt and pepper, and set aside.

3.Preheat the oven to 150 degrees Celsius. Preheat an oil-filled wide pan or deep-fryer to 190°C (a cube of bread will turn golden in 30 seconds when oil is hot enough). Deep-fry the fish in 4 batches for 1 minute or until golden and crisp. Drain on paper towels after removing with a slotted spoon. Place on a baking sheet and keep warm in the oven while you finish the rest of the fish.

4.While the last batch of fish is cooking, wrap tortillas in foil and steam them in the oven.

5.Add lettuce, fish, mango salsa, sour cream, hot sauce or chili, and extra coriander to the tortillas. Serve with lime wedges on the side.

SWORDFISH SKEWERS WITH CHILLI PEANUT DRESSING

Servings:4

INGREDIENTS

- 2/3 cup (165ml) soy sauce
- 2 tablespoons brown sugar
- 4 x 200g swordfish fillets, cut into 3cm pieces
- CHILLI PEANUT DRESSING
- 1/3 cup (80ml) peanut oil
- 8 red (Asian) eschalots, finely chopped
- 2 long red chillies, seeds removed, finely chopped
- 4 garlic cloves, finely chopped

- 3cm piece of ginger, grated
- 1/3 firmly packed cup (80g) brown sugar
- 2 tablespoons fish sauce
- Juice of 2 limes, plus wedges to serve
- 1/3 cup (50g) roasted unsalted peanuts, chopped
- 1/4 cup chopped coriander, plus extra leaves to serve

PREPARATION

1.Soak 8 wooden skewers for 30 minutes in cold water (or use metal skewers).

2.In a separate bowl, mix the soy sauce and sugar, stirring to dissolve the sugar, then add the fish. Set aside for 10 minutes to marinate.

3.Heat 1 tablespoon oil in a pan over medium heat for the dressing. Cook eschalot for 3-4 minutes, stirring occasionally, until golden. Cook, stirring continuously, for 1 minute or until the chili, garlic, and ginger are fragrant. Cook, stirring regularly, for 2-3 minutes, or until the sugar begins to caramelize. Remove from the heat and whisk in the fish sauce, lime juice, nuts, coriander, 1/4 cup (60ml) oil, and 1 1/2 tablespoons water. Taste and adjust the flavors to your liking; you should have a good mix of sweet, sour, salty, and hot flavors. Serve in a serving dish.

4.Preheat a chargrill pan or a barbecue to high heat. Using soaked skewers, thread the fish onto the skewers. Grill for 1-2 minutes on either hand, or until charred and finished.

5.Add coriander leaves to the swordfish skewers and serve with lime wedges and a chilli peanut dressing.

FISH COOKED IN A JAR WITH FENNEL AND ORANGE

Servings:4

INGREDIENTS

- 4 x 180g firm white fish fillets (such as ling)
- 8 lemon thyme sprigs
- 8 flat-leaf parsley sprigs
- 2 tablespoons olive oil
- 2 garlic cloves
- 8 whole black peppercorns
- 4 lemon slices
- 2 tablespoons white wine
- 400g can cannellini beans, rinsed, drained

- FENNEL AND ORANGE SALAD
- 2 small fennel bulbs, thinly sliced (a mandoline is ideal), fronds reserved
- Juice of 1/2 lemon
- 2 oranges, peeled, sliced
- 1 cup (120g) pitted kalamata olives
- 1/3 cup flat-leaf parsley leaves
- 1/4 cup (60ml) extra virgin olive oil

PREPARATION

1.Place 2 fish fillets in each jar, then divide the thyme, parsley, olive oil, garlic, peppercorns, lemon slices and wine between the jars. Close and seal the jar after seasoning with sea salt.

2.Bring a big pot of water to a rolling boil. Place the jars in the pan with care, ensuring that the water comes halfway up the sides. Reduce the heat to medium-low and continue to cook for another 20 minutes, or until the fish is opaque and cooked through.

3.Meanwhile, for the salad, combine all ingredients in a large bowl, season with sea salt and freshly ground black pepper and toss gently to combine.

4.Remove the jars from the pan with care and set aside for 5 minutes. Plate the salad, cannellini beans, and fish, then garnish with the reserved fennel fronds.

MOQUECA (BRAZILIAN FISH STEW)

Servings:6

INGREDIENTS

- 1kg skinless firm white fish fillet (such as snapper), pin-boned, cut into 3cm cubes
- 1/3 cup (80ml) lime juice
- 1/4 cup (60ml) olive oil
- 1 red onion, thinly sliced
- 1 green capsicum, thinly sliced
- 1 red capsicum, thinly sliced
- 3 garlic cloves, finely chopped
- 2 short red chillies, finely chopped

- 2 cups (500ml) fish stock
- 400g can chopped tomatoes
- 270ml can coconut milk
- 1 tablespoon virgin coconut oil (see note)
- 6 large green prawns, peeled (tails intact), deveined
- Coriander leaves and steamed rice, to serve

PREPARATION

1.Toss the fish with 2 teaspoons lime juice and 1 teaspoon sea salt in a large ceramic bowl. To marinate, chill for 30 minutes.

2.In a large saucepan, heat the olive oil over medium heat. Cook for 3 minutes, or until onion is softened.

3.Add the capsicum, garlic, and chili, and cook for another 5 minutes, or until the capsicum is softened, stirring occasionally.

4.In a large mixing bowl, combine the stock, tomatoes, coconut milk, and coconut oil. Bring to a boil, then reduce to medium and cook for 20-25 minutes, or until the liquid has slightly reduced.

5.Add the prawns, fish, and marinating juices, and cook for an additional 8-10 minutes, or until the seafood is just cooked through. Season to taste with the remaining 2 tablespoons lime juice. Serve with rice and coriander.

LEMON-CRUMBED FISH WITH FENNEL, PARSLEY AND CAPER SALAD

Servings:4

INGREDIENTS

- 1/4 cup (60ml) extra virgin olive oil, plus extra to drizzle
- 2 garlic cloves, finely chopped
- Finely grated zest of 2 lemons, plus lemon juice to drizzle
- 1 cup (70g) fresh breadcrumbs

- 2 tsp chopped lemon thyme or regular thyme leaves
- 2 tbs grated parmesan
- 4 x 200g skinless, boneless firm white fish fillets (such as blue-eye)
- 1 fennel bulb
- 50g baby spinach leaves
- 1/2 bunch flat-leaf parsley, leaves chopped
- 2 tbs baby capers, rinsed, drained

PREPARATION

1.Preheat the oven to 190 degrees Celsius. In an ovenproof frypan, heat 2 tablespoons oil over low heat. Cook for 2-3 minutes, or until garlic and zest are soft. Cook, stirring continuously, for 2-3 minutes, or until breadcrumbs are fully coated in oil (but not browned). Season with salt and pepper and move to a bowl with thyme and parmesan.

2.Wipe out the pan and heat the remaining 1 tablespoon of oil over medium heat. Cook for 1 minute before topping with the breadcrumb mixture (don't worry if any of it falls into the pan). Switch to the oven and bake for 8 minutes, or until the crumbs are golden and the fish is cooked through.

3.Remove from the oven, place on a plate, and set aside for 5 minutes to cool.

4.Prepare the salad while the fish is resting. Finely shave the fennel with a mandoline or a sharp knife. Combine the spinach, parsley, and capers in a mixing bowl. Season with salt and pepper, then drizzle with lemon juice and extra oil, tossing to mix.

5.Serve the fish with the fennel salad right away..

FISH AND CLAM CHOWDER

Servings:6

INGREDIENTS

- 1kg clams (vongole)
- 1 tablespoon olive oil
- 250g bacon, fat trimmed, cut into batons
- 1 onion, chopped
- 2 garlic cloves, finely chopped
- 2 tablespoons plain flour
- 1L (4 cups) fish stock
- Small bunch thyme leaves, tied with kitchen string
- 1 bay leaf
- 500g desiree potatoes, peeled, cut into 2-3cm pieces

- 1 cup (250ml) milk
- 1 cup (250ml) pure (thin) cream
- 500g skinless white fish fillets, deboned (such as ling or blue-eye), cut into 3cm pieces
- Finely chopped flat-leaf parsley and crusty bread, to serve

PREPARATION

To extract any grit, soak the clams in a bowl of cold water for 15 minutes. Drop from the method.

In a large saucepan, heat the oil over medium-high heat. Cook, stirring occasionally, for 3-4 minutes, or until fat has made. Cook for another 2-3 minutes, or until the onion and garlic are softened.

Toss in the flour and whisk to mix. Stir in the stock, thyme, bay leaf, and potato until all is well combined. It's that time of year. Reduce heat to medium-low and cook for 20 minutes, or until a small, sharp knife pierces the potato almost tender in the center.

After that, add the milk and cream, followed by the fish. Reduce to a low heat and cook for 8 minutes, or until the fish is just finished.

Drain the clams, return them to the pan, and cook for another 3-4 minutes, or until the clams are fully cooked and the shells have opened.

Season with freshly ground black pepper and ladle chowder into warm cups. Serve with crusty bread to mop up the liquid and garnished with parsley.

BAKED FISH WITH SALSA VERDE AND ROSEMARY POTATOES

Servings:4

INGREDIENTS

- 500g small waxy potatoes (such as Anya or coliban), thinly sliced (a mandoline is ideal)
- 1 lemon, thinly sliced (a mandoline is ideal), plus 2 tsp finely grated zest
- 2 tbs chopped rosemary
- 3/4 cup (185ml) olive oil
- 1 garlic clove

- 1 cup flat-leaf parsley
- 1 cup basil leaves
- 2 tbs capers, rinsed, drained
- 4 x 180g firm white fish fillets (such as blue eye)

PREPARATION

. Preheat the oven to 200 degrees Celsius.

Season potato, lemon slices, and rosemary with 1/4 cup (60ml) oil, then spread in a single layer in a roasting pan. 10 minutes in the oven

Meanwhile, finely cut garlic, parsley, basil, lemon zest, and capers in a food processor to produce salsa verde. Slowly drizzle the remaining 1/2 cup (125ml) olive oil into the mixture while the motor is working. Delete from the equation.

Remove the fish from the oven and put it on top of the roasting pan, with a lemon slice from the pan on top of each fillet. Season with salt and pepper, then bake for an additional 8 minutes, or until the fish is cooked through.

Serve with salsa verde drizzled on top.

SEAFOOD ANTIPASTI SALAD

Servings:4

INGREDIENTS

- 1/2 cup (125ml) white wine
- 1kg pot-ready mussels
- 2 small zucchinis
- 1 cup wild rocket leaves
- 12 cherry tomatoes, halved
- 1/3 cup (40g) pitted kalamata olives
- 1 tablespoon capers, rinsed, drained
- 12 cooked prawns, peeled (tails intact), deveined
- 1/2 cup (100g) store-bought roasted red capsicum strips
- 4 artichoke hearts in brine, rinsed, halved
- 4 grissini (thin breadsticks)

- Lemon wedges, to serve

PREPARATION

. In a large saucepan over high heat, bring the wine to a boil. Cook for 2 minutes, shaking the pan occasionally, after inserting the mussels. Any mussels that have opened should be transferred to a wide bowl, then cover and cook for another 1-2 minutes, shaking the pan occasionally, until all the mussels have opened. Place the mussels in a bowl and set aside.

Slice zucchinis into long, thin ribbons with a vegetable peeler or mandoline, then combine with rocket, tomatoes, olives, and capers in a cup. Season with salt and pepper and toss to mix.

4 plates with mussels, prawns, capsicum, artichoke, and zucchini salad Serve with lemon wedges and grissini.

CONCLUSION

PROVIDES OMEGA-3 FATTY ACIDS

One of the main reasons fish is so good for us is because it contains high levels of omega-3 fatty acids. In a world where most people consume far too many omega-6 fatty acids from refined vegetable oils, salad dressings, and processed spices, increasing omega-3 foods is urgently needed.

Omega-3 fatty acids act as a counterbalance to omega-6 fats and help keep inflammation down by balancing the levels of omega-3 and omega-6 fatty acids. Omega-3 fatty acids are considered to be anti-inflammatory, while omega-6 fatty acids are anti-inflammatory. We need both types, but many people lack omega-3 fatty acids. Consuming higher omega-3 levels has been linked to better mental health, lower triglyceride levels, improved reproductive health and fertility, better hormone control, and a lower risk of diabetes.

HELPS IN LOWERING INFLAMMATION

The reason the omega-3s found in fish are so valuable is mainly because of their ability to fight inflammation. They help control inflammatory diseases that lead to numerous diseases, including cancer, rheumatoid arthritis, and asthma.

Both types of polyunsaturated fats described above play an important role in the body and contribute to the formation of our hormones, cell membranes and immune

responses. But omega-3 and omega-6 fatty acids have opposite effects when it comes to inflammation. In general, too much omega-6 and too little omega-3 cause inflammation. Inflammation is believed to contribute to the development of chronic conditions like cancer, diabetes, heart disease, and more.

PROMOTES HEART HEALTH

EPA and DHA are two omega-3 fatty acids that are essential for controlling inflammation and promoting heart health. Studies show that daily consumption of EPA and DHA can help reduce the risk of heart disease and death from heart disease, sometimes as effective as prescription drugs like statins. The combination of nutrients in seafood also helps regulate the heartbeat, lower blood pressure and cholesterol, reduce blood clot formation, and lower triglycerides. All of these can help protect against heart disease and stroke.

CAN HELP PROTECT AGAINST CANCER

Research shows that eating more fish and seafood high in omega-3s benefits the immune system and helps fight cancer by suppressing inflammation. While a vegetarian diet has been linked to a lower incidence of certain types of cancer (such as colon cancer), pescatarianism is associated with an even lower risk compared to vegetarians and non-vegetarians, according to some studies.

Several studies also suggest that consuming plenty of omega-3 fatty acids may help those previously diagnosed with cancer by stopping tumor growth. A pescatarian lifestyle high in omega-3s can also help people undergoing chemotherapy or other cancer treatments, as they help maintain muscle mass and regulate inflammatory responses that are already compromised in cancer patients.

COMBATS COGNITIVE DECLINE

Omega-3 fatty acids like DHA are vital for proper brain development and maintenance of cognitive function in old age. Many studies have shown that low omega-3 levels in the elderly are linked to several markers of impaired brain function, including dementia or Alzheimer's disease. Lower omega-3 levels during pregnancy have even been linked to children who have lower memory test scores and learning difficulties.

BOOSTS THE MOOD

Because they fight oxidative stress, which affects the proper functioning of the brain, the omega-3s from fish and seafood have been linked to better mental health and a lower risk of dementia, depression, anxiety, and ADHD. This means that a Pescatarian diet can be a natural anti-anxiety remedy and help manage the symptoms of ADHD while fighting off symptoms of depression.

SUPPORTS WEIGHT LOSS

Many people have started using the Pescatarian diet for weight loss, and for good reason. Low intake of omega-3

fatty acids has been linked to obesity and weight gain. Studies also show that people who eat more plant-based foods (including vegetarians) tend to have lower BMIs and better weight management, probably because they eat more fiber and fewer calories.

Not only that, but healthy proteins and fats are critical to feeling full, and many of the nutrients found in fish can help reduce cravings. Regardless of your diet, aim for a high intake of fruits, vegetables, high quality proteins, healthy fats, seeds, nuts, fiber, and phytochemicals. All of these can help you lose weight quickly and keep it off.

The Pescatarian Cookbook for Beginners

+50 Delicious Simple Seafood Recipes

Johan Castillo

INTRODUCTION

A pescatarian diet is a flexible vegetarian diet that includes fish and other seafood. When you add fish to a vegetarian diet, you reap the following benefits:

Fish protein increases satiety as compared to beef and chicken. This means you will feel full quickly and not overeat. If you are looking to shed some pounds, it's the right time to start being on a pescatarian diet.

Calcium is extremely important for your bone health. Merely eating vegetables does not provide your body with enough calcium. But adding fish to a vegetarian diet does

Fatty fish are great sources of omega-3 fatty acids. These acids help lower inflammation in the body, which, in turn, reduces the risk of obesity, diabetes, and heart disease.

Compared to other animal proteins, consuming fish contributes lesser to greenhouse gas emission. So, you can protect the environment and your health.

For some, just eating vegetables, fruit, and nuts can be boring. Adding fish or any other seafood helps improve the taste and overall mood of lunch and/or dinner.

Many people are allergic to eggs, lactose intolerant, or may want to avoid eating meat or dairy products. For them, fish can be a good source of complete protein, calcium, and healthy fats.

WHAT DO PESCATARIANS EAT?

SEAFOOD: Mackerel, bass, haddock, salmon, tuna, Hilsa, sardines, Pomfret, carps, cod, caviar, mussels, crayfish, oyster, prawns, lobster, crab, squid, and scallops.

VEGETABLES: Spinach, chard, radish greens, carrot greens, Bengal gram greens, beetroot, carrot, broccoli, cauliflower, cabbage, Chinese cabbage, sweet potato, radish, turnip, parsnip, kale, cucumber, and tomato.

FRUITS: Apple, banana, avocado, strawberries, blackberries, mulberries, blueberries, gooseberries, pineapple, papaya, dragon fruit, passion fruit, watermelon, muskmelon, guava, peach, pear, pluot, plum, and mango.

PROTEIN: Kidney beans, lentils, fish, mushroom, Bengal gram, sprouts, black-eyed peas, cowpeas, garbanzo beans, soybean, soy milk, edamame, and tofu.

WHOLE GRAINS: Brown rice, barley, broken wheat, sorghum, multigrain bread, and multigrain flour.

FATS & OILS: Olive oil, avocado oil, fish oil, ghee, sunflower butter, and rice bran oil.

Nuts & Seeds Almonds, walnuts, pistachios, macadamia, pine nuts, hazelnuts, sunflower seeds, melon seeds, pumpkin seeds, chia seeds, and flaxseeds.

Herbs & Spices Cilantro, dill, fennel, parsley, oregano, thyme, bay leaf, chili flakes, chili powder, Kashmiri red chili powder, turmeric, coriander, cumin, mustard seeds, English mustard, mustard paste, star anise, saffron, cardamom, clove, garlic, cinnamon, ginger, mace, nutmeg, Allspice, onion powder, garlic powder, and ginger powder.

BEVERAGES: Water, coconut water, detox" water>, and freshly pressed fruit/vegetable juices.

With these ingredients, you can easily come up with a diet plan that's nutritionally balanced. Take a look at this sample pescatarian diet plan.

SMOKED FISH CAKES WITH NASTURTIUM CRUMBS

Servings:12

INGREDIENTS

- 500g undyed smoked cod
- 2 cups (500ml) milk
- 1 bay leaf
- 1 tbs sunflower oil, plus extra to deep-fry
- 1 onion, finely chopped
- 1 garlic clove, finely chopped
- 500g pontiac or Desiree potatoes, peeled, quartered
- 30g unsalted butter

- 2 eggs, lightly beaten
- 1 egg yolk, extra
- 20 nasturtium flowers and leaves
- 2 cups (100g) panko breadcrumbs
- 1 1/4 cups (100g) grated parmesan
- 2 cups (300g) plain flour, seasoned
- 1 cup (300g) whole-egg mayonnaise
- 2 tbs lemon juice

PREPARATION

1. Place the fish, flesh-side down, in a wide frypan with the milk and bay leaf, and poach for 6 minutes or until tender over medium-low heat. Remove the bay leaf and strain into a cup, reserving the poaching liquid. Delete from the equation.

2. In the meantime, heat oil in a frypan over medium heat and cook onion and garlic until soft, around 1-2 minutes.

3. Bring a saucepan of cold salted water to a boil over medium-high heat with the potato in it. Cook for 12 minutes, or until the vegetables are tender. Drain, then mash with butter and just enough of the reserved fish poaching liquid to moisten the mixture while keeping it stiff. Season with salt and pepper, then add the onion mixture and egg yolk. Flake the fish and add it to the potato mixture, discarding the skin and any bones. Make 12 patties out of the mixture.

4. Reserve 10 nasturtium flowers for the salad, then tear the rest into small bits and toss with breadcrumbs (or briefly pulse flowers and breadcrumbs in a small food processor). Stir in the parmesan cheese until it is well combined.

5. Coat fish cakes in seasoned flour, shake off excess, then in beaten egg, followed by breadcrumb mixture. To firm up, relax for 15 minutes.

6. In the meantime, make a loose dressing with mayonnaise, lemon juice, and a little warm water. In a cup, combine the nasturtium leaves and reserved flowers. Delete from the equation.

7. Pour half of the oil into a deep-fryer or large saucepan and heat to 190°C (a cube of bread will turn golden in 30 seconds when the oil is hot enough). Deep-fry the fish cakes in batches for 1 1/2 minutes or until golden. Drain on paper towels and keep warm until the rest of the fish cakes are ready.

8. To drizzle, serve warm fish cakes with a nasturtium salad and lemon mayonnaise..

TERIYAKI FISH PARCELS

Servings:4

INGREDIENTS

- 2 tbs mirin
- 2 tbs sake
- 1/4 cup (60ml) dark soy sauce
- 2 tsp honey
- 4cm piece ginger, grated
- 4 x 150g ling fillets (or other firm white fish fillets)
- 200g shiitake mushrooms, sliced
- 200g frozen podded edamame, skins removed
- 2/3 cup (25g) bean sprouts
- Coriander leaves, to serve

PREPARATION

1.In a mixing bowl, combine the mirin, sake, soy, honey, and ginger; pour over the fish and marinate for 30 minutes.

2.Preheat a high-heat barbecue (with a lid) or an oven to 225°C. Remove the fish from the marinade and set aside 1/3 cup (80ml). Place two 50cm squares of foil on top of each other for each parcel, then one 50cm square of baking paper on top of that. To make a mug, fold the ends of the foil over the paper. In the center of each cup, put a piece of fish, scatter with mushrooms, and drizzle with 1 tablespoon of the reserved marinade. To make a parcel, gather the ends of the baking paper and foil together. Place on a barbecue grill and close the lid, or bake for 15 minutes or until cooked through in the oven.

3.In the meantime, put the edamame in a bowl, cover with boiling water, and set aside for 5 minutes to soak. Drain the water.

4.To eat, scatter edamame, bean sprouts, and coriander leaves over the trout.

SMOKED TROUT FISHCAKES WITH PEA AND WATERCRESS SALAD

Servings:4

INGREDIENTS

- 800g Desiree potatoes, peeled, chopped
- Finely grated zest and juice of 1 lemon, plus extra wedges to serve
- 1/4 cup chopped chives, plus extra to serve
- 300g smoked ocean trout, roughly chopped
- 200g creme fraiche
- 2 eggs, lightly beaten with 1 tbs water

- 1/2 cup (50g) dried breadcrumbs
- Olive oil, to shallow-fry, plus extra to drizzle
- 1 tsp Dijon mustard
- 1 tbs apple cider vinegar
- 1 cup (160g) fresh peas
- 1 bunch watercress

PREPARATION

1.In a large saucepan of cold salted water, put the potatoes. Bring to a boil, then reduce to medium-high heat and cook for 15-20 minutes, or until the vegetables are tender. Return to the pan after draining. Heat for 30 seconds, stirring continuously, to remove any excess water. Enable to cool slightly before mashing coarsely.

2.In a mixing bowl, combine the lemon zest, chives, ocean trout, and 2 tablespoons creme fraiche.

3.Salt and pepper to taste, then cover and chill for 15 minutes.

4.Make 12 balls out of the mixture and flatten slightly to make 3cm-thick patties. Roll in breadcrumbs after coating with egg wash.

5.Heat 2cm oil in a frypan over medium heat and shallow-fry the fishcakes in batches for 1 1/2 minutes per side or until golden and crisp. Using a paper towel, absorb excess liquid and keep warm.

6.In a separate cup, whisk together the Dijon mustard, apple cider vinegar, and remaining creme fraiche, season to taste, and set aside. In a mixing dish, combine peas and watercress. Season with salt and pepper after drizzling with lemon juice and olive oil.

7.Serve fishcakes with salad, creme fraiche sauce, lemon wedges, and additional chives on the side.

THAI FISH PIE

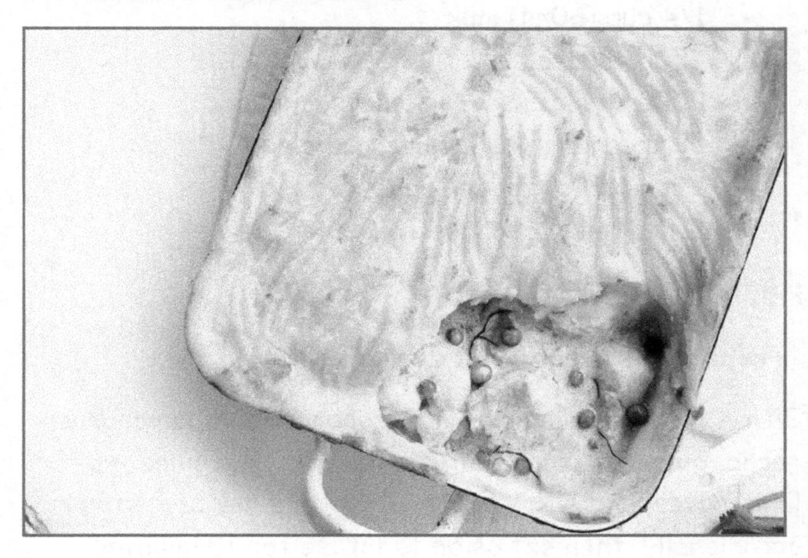

S

Servings:4

INGREDIENTS

- 400ml can coconut milk
- 1 lemongrass stalk (inner core only)
- 2 garlic cloves, finely chopped
- 2cm piece ginger, grated
- 2 tsp grated palm sugar
- 1 long red chilli, seeds removed, chopped
- 2 tsp fish sauce
- Juice of 1/2 lime
- 4 kaffir lime leaves, 2 shredded
- 2 tbs green curry paste
- 1.2kg pontiac potatoes, roughly chopped

- 80g unsalted butter, plus extra to dot
- 1/4 cup (60ml) milk
- 250g skinless ling fillets, chopped
- 250g skinless salmon fillets, chopped
- 16 green prawns, peeled, deveined
- 1 cup (120g) frozen peas, thawed
- 2 tbs finely chopped coriander leaves

PREPARATION

1.Preheat the oven to 180 degrees Celsius.

2.In a medium saucepan, add coconut milk, lemongrass, garlic, ginger, sugar, chili, fish sauce, lime juice, kaffir lime leaves, and curry paste. Bring to a low boil, stirring occasionally, then set aside to infuse for 10 minutes.

3.Place the potato in a saucepan of cold salted water over high heat in the meantime. Bring to a boil, then reduce to a low heat and cook for 12 minutes, or until the vegetables are tender. Drain and mash the potatoes, then add the butter and milk, season with salt and pepper, and beat with a wooden spoon until smooth and fluffy.

4.In a 1.2L baking dish, combine the tuna, prawns, and peas. Remove and discard the lemongrass and whole lime leaves from the sauce. Pour over the seafood after applying the coriander.

5.Dot with extra butter and top with mashed potato, raking the surface with a fork.

6.Bake for 25-30 minutes, or until the top is golden and the seafood is cooked.

FRENCH-STYLE FISH STEW

S

Servings:6

INGREDIENTS

- 1/4 cup (60ml) olive oil
- 6 large green prawns, peeled (tails intact), deveined, shells reserved
- 150ml white wine
- 200ml good-quality fish stock
- 1 small fennel bulb, finely chopped
- 1 onion, finely chopped
- 3 garlic cloves, thinly sliced
- 1 desiree potato, chopped
- Pared zest of 1 orange
- 1 bay leaf

- 2 tsp chopped thyme leaves
- 1 tbs harissa
- 2 tbs tomato puree
- 400g can chopped tomatoes
- 12 mussels, debearded
- 200g firm boneless fish, cut into 3cm pieces
- 1/2 cup (150g) whole-egg mayonnaise
- 2 tbs chopped flat-leaf parsley leaves
- Baguette, to serve

PREPARATION

1.In a wide frypan, heat 1 tablespoon of oil over medium-high heat. Fry the prawn shells until they turn pink, around 1-2 minutes. Cook for 2-3 minutes, or until the wine has been reduced by half. Bring the stock to a low boil, then strain and set aside.

2.In a frypan, heat the remaining 2 tbsp oil over medium heat. Season with salt and pepper, then reduce heat to low and add the fennel, onion, and garlic.

3.Cook for 10 minutes, or until vegetables are softened, wrapped.

4.In the meantime, cook the potato for 10 minutes or until almost tender in a saucepan of boiling, salted water, then drain.

5.Toss the onion mixture with the orange zest, bay leaf, thyme, and half of the harissa. The potato, tomato puree, canned tomato, and strained stock are then added. Season after 10 minutes of simmering or until slightly reduced.

6.Bring to a boil the peeled prawns, mussels, and fish. Cover and cook for 3 minutes, or until the mussels have opened and the seafood is just cooked.

7.Combine mayonnaise and remaining harissa in a mixing bowl. Serve the stew with baguette and mayonnaise, garnished with parsley.

THAI RED FISH CURRY WITH NOODLES

Servings:4

INGREDIENTS

- 200g Pad Thai rice noodles
- 1/4 cup (60ml) peanut oil
- 600g firm boneless white fish fillets (such as ling), cut into 2cm thick slices
- 2 garlic cloves, finely chopped
- 1/2 bunch spring onions, chopped, dark and pale parts separated
- 1 bunch coriander, leaves picked, roots chopped
- 1/4 cup (60ml) Thai red curry paste
- 1 tablespoon fish sauce

- 150g sugar snap peas
- 2/3 cup (165ml) coconut cream
- 1/2 cup (75g) chopped peanuts
- Bean sprouts, to serve
- Lime wedges, to serve

PREPARATION

1.Soak noodles for 10 minutes in hot water or until tender, then drain. Delete from the equation.

2.Season the fish with 1 tablespoon oil in a wok over high heat. Half of the fish should be stir-fried for 2 minutes or until golden, then transferred to a tray. Repeat with the remaining fish and 1 tbsp oil.

3.In a separate pan, heat the remaining 1 tablespoon oil and add the garlic, white spring onion, and coriander root. Stir-fry for 1-2 minutes, or until the vegetables are softened. Stir in the curry paste for another 2 minutes, or until fragrant, then add the fish sauce, sugar snap peas, and 1/4 cup (60ml) water, and cook for another 2 minutes, or until the sauce has slightly reduced. Return the fish to the wok, along with the remaining spring onion and coconut cream, and toss to mix and warm through.

4.Toss the noodle mixture into four bowls and cover with the fish curry. Serve with coriander leaves, peanuts, bean sprouts, and lime wedges right away.

BLACKENED FISH WITH SWEET POTATO CHIPS

Servings:4

INGREDIENTS

- 4 x 180g blue-eye fillets, skin removed
- 30g unsalted butter, melted
- 2 tbs Cajun spice mix
- 1/3 cup (80ml) olive oil
- 800g sweet potato, cut into chips
- 1 1/2 tsp caster sugar
- Aioli, coriander leaves and lemon wedges, to serve

PREPARATION

1.Brush the fish with butter, season with salt and pepper, and sprinkle with the Cajun spice blend. Enable 30 minutes for marinating.

2.Preheat the oven to 220°C. Drizzle the chips with 1/4 cup (60ml) oil, then season with salt and sugar. Bake for 25 minutes, turning halfway, or until crisp, on a rack placed above a baking tray.

3.In a separate frypan, heat the remaining 1 tbsp oil over medium-high heat. Cook for 6-8 minutes, turning once, until fish is finished. On the side, serve the fish with chips, aioli, coriander, and lemon wedges..

FISH BANH MI WITH QUICK PICKLED VEGETABLES

Servings:4

INGREDIENTS

- 1 teaspoon ground turmeric
- 2 tablespoons plain flour
- 1/3 cup (80ml) milk
- 2 tablespoons fresh dill, chopped
- 500g firm boneless white fish fillets (such as blue eye), cut into 2cm pieces
- 2 tablespoons coconut oil
- 1 thick baguette, split
- 1 Lebanese cucumber, thinly sliced

- 1 cup fresh coriander
- 1 cup Thai basil leaves
- 1 lime, halved
- QUICK PICKLED VEGETABLES
- 1/3 cup (75g) coconut sugar
- 1/3 cup (80ml) rice vinegar
- 1 carrot, cut into matchsticks
- 1 small daikon (Asian white radish), cut into matchsticks

PREPARATION

1.Combine sugar and vinegar in a small saucepan over low heat, stirring until the sugar dissolves, then set aside to cool for the simple pickled vegetables. Set aside for another 30 minutes to pickle the carrots and daikon, then drain.

2.In a separate bowl, mix the turmeric and flour, then season. In a separate dish, combine the milk and dill. Shake off any excess flour after dipping the fish in the milk mixture and then in the flour mixture.

3.In a medium-sized frypan, heat the oil. Cook the fish in batches for 3-4 minutes, rotating once, or until golden.

4. Brush the interior of the baguette with a little of the pan's oil. Place the tuna, cucumber, pickled vegetables, coriander, and Thai basil on the baguette. To serve, squeeze lime juice over the top..

CURED KINGFISH WITH PICKLED BABY BEETROOT

S

Servings:4

INGREDIENTS

- 1 tsp each black peppercorns, coriander seeds and fennel seeds, crushed
- 1/2 cup (110g) sea salt fakes
- 1/2 cup (110g) caster sugar
- 1/2 cup chopped dill, plus sprigs to serve
- 500g skinless sashimi-grade kingfish fillet
- 100g sour cream
- 1/3 cup (80ml) milk
- 2 tsp lemon juice

- Flat-leaf parsley leaves, to serve
- PICKLED BABY BEETROOT
- 1/3 cup (80ml) white wine vinegar
- 2 bay leaves
- 1 tsp coriander seeds
- 2 tbs caster sugar
- 3 tsp lime juice
- 1 bunch raw baby beetroot, peeled, very thinly sliced

PREPARATION

1.In a mixing bowl, combine the spices, salt, sugar, and dill. Turn the fish to coat it in the sauce. Refrigerate for 3-4 hours, covered. Rinse thoroughly and pat dry.

2.In a pan over medium heat, mix vinegar, bay, coriander seeds, sugar, 1/3 cup (80ml) water, and 2 tsp salt for the beetroot. Bring to a boil, then turn off the heat and add the lime. Pour the pickling liquid over the beets in a dish. Season with salt and pepper. Allow to pickle for 2 hours. Drain the water.

3.In a mixing bowl, combine the sour cream, milk, and lemon juice. It's that time of year.

4.Thinly slice the fish and serve with a seasoning drizzled beetroot, dill, and parsley..

CURED TROUT WITH FENNEL SALAD AND FISH CRACKLING

Servings:4

INGREDIENTS

- 500g rainbow or freshwater trout, filleted (leaving skin intact), pin-boned
- 1/2 cup (110g) caster sugar
- 150g sea salt fakes
- 1/4 bunch dill, finely chopped
- Finely grated zest of 1 1/2 lemons, plus juice of 1 lemon
- Sunflower oil, to deep-fry
- 1 baby fennel, fronds reserved

- 2 tbs olive oil
- 1 Lebanese cucumber, peeled, finely chopped
- 1 tbs baby capers, rinsed, drained
- 100g creme fraiche

PREPARATION

1.Remove the skin from the fillets of trout, then trim and scrape the skin clean. Cover the skin in plastic wrap and place it in the refrigerator until ready to use.

2.In a mixing bowl, combine the sugar, salt, dill, and half of the lemon zest. Place half of the sugar mixture on a large piece of plastic wrap on a work surface. Cover with the remaining mixture and place the trout on top. Place in a baking dish, tightly wrapped in plastic wrap (the cure may draw out liquid). Enable to chill overnight.

3.Preheat the oven to 75°C the next day. Place the skins on a baking tray lined with parchment paper. Bake for 30 minutes or until crisp, then cut each piece of skin into quarters with kitchen scissors.

4.Heat a small saucepan half-filled with sunflower oil to 190°C (a cube of bread will turn golden in 30 seconds). Crisp the skins in a deep fryer for 1 minute. Set aside after draining on paper towels and seasoning with salt.

5.Using a mandoline, finely shave the fennel, then toss with olive oil and lemon juice. Rinse the trout under cold running water after removing it from the plastic wrap. Using a paper towel, pat dry. Trout can be cut into 1cm bits with a sharp knife.

6.Combine the trout, cucumber, capers, and the remaining lemon zest in a mixing bowl. Serve with creme fraiche, crackling, and reserved fennel fronds on top of the fennel salad and trout mixture.

BRUSSELS SPROUTS WITH FISH SAUCE VINAIGRETTE

Servings:4

INGREDIENTS

- Sunflower oil, to deep-fry
- 500g Brussels sprouts, halved
- 1/4 bunch coriander, leaves picked
- 1/4 cup finely chopped mint leaves
- FISH SAUCE VINAIGRETTE
- 1/4 cup (60ml) fish sauce
- 1 tbs rice vinegar
- 1/2 lime, charred, juiced
- 1 1/2 tbs caster sugar

- 1 garlic clove, crushed
- 1 each small red chilli and small green chilli, thinly sliced

PREPARATION

1.To make the vinaigrette, whisk together all of the ingredients in a bowl with 2 tablespoons water.

2.Heat an oil-filled deep-fryer or large saucepan to 180°C. Cook the Brussels sprouts, in batches of 2-3, for 1-2 minutes, until the outside leaves are dark brown and the sprouts are tender. Using a paper towel, absorb excess liquid.

3.To serve, mix the sprouts, coriander, and mint on a serving plate with 1/3 cup (80ml) vinaigrette and gently toss to combine.

SOUPE DE POISSON (FISH SOUP)

S

Servings:6

INGREDIENTS

- 2 tablespoons olive oil
- 2 onions, roughly chopped
- 2 leeks (pale part only), chopped
- 1kg mixed seafood (such as whole prawns, salmon and blue-eye)
- 1 fennel bulb, chopped
- 4 tomatoes, chopped
- 2 garlic cloves, chopped

- 2 flat-leaf parsley sprigs, plus chopped parsley to serve
- 2 bay leaves
- 1 long strip pared orange rind
- 1 tablespoon tomato paste
- 1L (4 cups) good-quality fish stock
- 2 cups (500ml) Provencal fish soup or canned lobster bisque
- 1/2 cup (125ml) thickened cream
- Cheesy toasts and saffron mayonnaise (optional), to serve

PREPARATION

1.In a large saucepan, heat the oil over medium heat. Cook, stirring periodically, for 2-3 minutes, or until the onion and leek begin to soften. Stir in the seafood, fennel, tomato, garlic, and parsley for 2 minutes. Stir in the bay leaves, orange rind, and tomato paste, then pour in the fish supply. Bring to a boil over high heat, then reduce to low heat and cook for 30 minutes, or until the fish fillets have broken down. To remove the flavor, strain through a sieve when pressing down on the solids.

2.Return the stock to the pan with the fish soup or lobster bisque and cook for 10 minutes over medium heat, until slightly reduced. Stir in the milk, then cook for 1 minute, or until thoroughly heated. Season, then ladle into warm bowls, top with extra parsley, toasts, and mayonnaise, if desired.

PAN-FRIED FISH WITH HERB SAUCE

Servings:4

INGREDIENTS

- 1 large lemon
- 3 garlic cloves, sliced
- 1 cup flat-leaf parsley leaves, torn
- 12 each mint and basil leaves, torn
- 1/4 cup oregano leaves
- 1/3 cup (80ml) extra virgin olive oil
- 4 x 180g white fish fillets with skin on (such as blue-eye or snapper)
- Crusty bread, to serve

PREPARATION

1. Preheat the oven to 180 degrees Celsius. With a peeler, peel the lemon rind, being careful not to take any of the white pith. In a tub, squeeze the lemon juice. Apply the garlic, spices, and half of the oil to the pan. Put aside after seasoning.

2.In an ovenproof pan, heat the remaining oil over medium-high heat. 30 seconds of frying lemon rind Season the fish, then put it in the pan skin-side down. Cook for 3-4 minutes over medium heat, until the skin is crisp and the flesh has turned white around the edges. Preheat the oven to 350°F and bake the pan for 5 minutes, or until the fish is just cooked through. Return the pan to a low heat environment, pour in the herb mixture, and heat through. Fish should be served with crusty bread..

PROVENCALE KINGFISH

S

Servings:4

INGREDIENTS

- 4 x 180g kingfish fillets with skin on
- 1 1/2 tablespoons olive oil
- 2 garlic cloves, finely chopped
- Grated zest of 1 lemon
- 600g vine-ripened tomatoes, seeds removed, chopped
- 2 anchovy fillets in oil, drained, chopped
- 2 tablespoons capers, rinsed, drained
- 2 teaspoons red wine vinegar
- 1 teaspoon caster sugar
- 50g pitted kalamata olives

- 2 tablespoons flat-leaf parsley leaves
- 2 cups baby spinach or rocket

PREPARATION

1.Preheat the oven to 350°F and season the kingfish with salt and pepper.

2.In a medium-high-heat frypan, heat 2 teaspoons oil. Cook for 3 minutes with the skin side down, then turn and cook for another 3 minutes or until fish is cooked through. Place on a plate and cover with foil to keep warm as you prepare the sauce.

3.In the same pan, heat the remaining oil over low heat. Stir in the garlic, lemon zest, and a pinch of salt and pepper for 2-3 minutes, or until soft but not browned. Toss in the tomato, anchovies, capers, vinegar, and sugar, and cover partially. Cook for 3-4 minutes, or until the tomato has softened. Add the olives and parsley and mix well..

FISHCAKES WITH PEA CRUSH

S

Servings:4

INGREDIENTS

- 1 cup mashed potato (2 large potatoes)
- 210g can pink salmon, drained, skin and bones discarded
- 210g can tuna in oil, drained
- 1 small onion, finely chopped
- 1 garlic clove, finely chopped
- 1 tablespoon Dijon mustard
- Grated zest of 1 lemon, plus wedges to squeeze
- 2 tablespoons finely chopped flat-leaf parsley
- 2 eggs
- 1/2 cup (125ml) milk

- 1 cup (150g) plain flour
- 200g panko breadcrumbs
- Sunflower oil, to shallow-fry
- 3 cups (360g) frozen peas
- 30g unsalted butter

PREPARATION

1.In a mixing bowl, combine the potato, salmon, tuna, onion, garlic, mustard, lemon zest, parsley, and a pinch of salt and pepper. Shape the mixture into 12 small logs, each about 6cm long, with your hands. To firm up, chill for 20 minutes.

2.In a small cup, whisk together the eggs and milk. Season the flour with salt and pepper in a separate dish. In a separate bowl, position the breadcrumbs. To coat the fishcakes, first dip them in flour, then in the egg mixture, and finally in breadcrumbs.

3.In a medium-high-heat pan, heat 3cm sunflower oil. In batches, shallow-fry the fishcakes for 3-4 minutes, rotating once, until crisp and golden.

4.In the meantime, boil the peas in salted water for 5 minutes, or until tender. Return to the pan with the butter after draining well. Season with salt and pepper, then mash with a potato masher gently.

5.Serve the fishcakes with lemon halves and crushed peas.

THAI FISH AND PUMPKIN

S

Servings:4

INGREDIENTS

- 1 tablespoon sunflower oil
- 3 tablespoons Thai red curry paste
- 200ml light coconut milk
- 3 cups (750ml) salt-reduced chicken or fish stock
- 4 Asian (red) eschalots, thinly sliced
- 1 long red chilli, thinly sliced
- 2 kaffir lime leaves, finely shredded (optional)
- 250g pumpkin, peeled, cut into 2cm pieces
- 1 green capsicum, cut into strips

- 2 tablespoons tamarind puree
- 2 tablespoons fish sauce
- 1 tablespoon brown sugar
- 600g skinless chunky fish fillets (such as blue eye, ling or snapper), cut into 3cm pieces
- 100g baby spinach leaves

PREPARATION

1.In a saucepan, heat the oil over medium-high heat. Cook, stirring constantly, for 2 minutes or until fragrant.

2.In a large mixing bowl, combine the coconut milk, stock, eschalot, chili, and kaffir lime leaves, if using. Cook for 20 minutes, or until the pumpkin is tender, with the pumpkin, capsicum, tamarind, fish sauce, sugar, and a pinch of salt.

3.Add the fish and cook for 5 minutes, or until opaque.

4.Toss half of the spinach into four warm bowls with the fish and vegetables. Scatter the remaining spinach on top, then drizzle with the sauce and serve..

ASIAN-STYLE FISH BAKED IN A BANANA LEAF

Servings:2

INGREDIENTS

- 1 large fresh banana leaf (see Notes)
- 800g whole snapper (or red emperor), cleaned
- 1 tablespoon Thai red curry paste or laksa paste
- 2 tablespoons coconut cream (use the thick cream from the top of a can of coconut milk)
- 2 tablespoons finely shredded ginger
- 8 kaffir lime leaves, thinly shredded (see Notes)
- 2 tablespoons coriander sprigs
- 1 long red chilli, sliced on an angle
- 2 cups steamed white medium grain rice, to serve

- DRESSING
- 3 slices fresh lime or lemon
- 2 tablespoons fish sauce
- 1/4 cup (60ml) lime juice
- 2 tablespoons sweet chilli sauce

PREPARATION

1.Preheat the oven to 180 degrees Celsius. Wash the banana leaf and cut off just enough to encase the fish, reserving some for serving.

2.Place a square of foil on the banana leaf that is slightly larger than the fish, then top with the fish. In the thickest section of the flesh, make two slashes. Spread curry paste on the fish, then cover with coconut cream. Sprinkle with ginger and lime leaves, then wrap the fish in the leaf, head and tail at opposite ends of the 'tube,' and tie with kitchen string.

3.Place the parcel in a roasting pan and bake for 40 minutes, or until cooked through (open the leaf and run a knife along the backbone to check). It's done when the flesh quickly separates from the bone.)

4.In the meantime, make the dressing by slicing the lime into small wedges and combining it with the fish sauce, lime juice, and sweet chilli sauce.

5.If desired, place the banana leaf on a platter lined with fresh banana leaf. Serve with rice and a dollop of dressing, garnished with coriander and chili.

SUNDAY ROAST FISH

S

Servings:4

INGREDIENTS

- 1 bunch baby (Dutch) carrots, peeled
- 4 small parsnips, peeled, halved
- 8 garlic cloves (unpeeled)
- 4 rosemary sprigs, plus extra chopped rosemary (or parsley) to serve
- 2 tablespoons olive oil
- 100g small shiitake mushrooms, trimmed
- 4 x 200g blue eye fillets (or other firm white fish)
- 16 baby brussels sprouts (or 8 small), halved, blanched for 2 minutes

- 2 tablespoons balsamic vinegar (optional)

PREPARATION

1.Preheat the oven to 200 degrees Celsius.

2.In a roasting pan, arrange carrots, parsnips, garlic, and 4 rosemary sprigs, then drizzle with 1 tablespoon oil and season. Toss all together well, then bake for 20-25 minutes.

3.Add the mushrooms to the pan and toss them again with 1 tablespoon of oil. Bake for 15 minutes, or until vegetables are golden brown and almost tender, turning once or twice.

4.Preheat a finely oiled frypan over high heat in the meantime. Cook the fish for 1-2 minutes, skin-side down, until golden and crisp. Season the fish and place it skin-side up in a roasting pan. Attach the sprouts and bake for 6-8 minutes, or until the fish is finished.

5.To eat, throw out the baked rosemary and divide the fish, vegetables, and garlic between warm plates. If needed, drizzle with balsamic vinegar and top with chopped rosemary or parsley. The garlic should be warm and ready to be squeezed out into the plate's juices.

FISH AND PRAWN TAGINE WITH APRICOTS

Servings:4

INGREDIENTS

- 100g dried apricots
- 400g can cherry tomatoes
- 1 teaspoon ground cumin
- 1/2 teaspoon each turmeric and paprika
- 2 cinnamon quills
- 600g skinless mahi mahi or swordfish fillets, cut into 2-3cm cubes
- 8 green prawns, peeled (tails intact), deveined
- 1 cup (200g) couscous
- 2 tablespoons flat-leaf parsley leaves

- 4 lemon wedges

PREPARATION

1.To soak the apricots, place them in a small bowl, cover with 200ml boiling water, and set aside for 30 minutes.

2.Preheat a pan over medium heat and add the tomatoes. Cumin, turmeric, paprika, and cinnamon can be added now. Season to taste. Stir in the apricots and their soaking liquid, then bring to a boil over medium-high heat.

3.Add the fish and prawns, and cook for 5-10 minutes over medium heat, until the broth is soupy and the fish and prawns are cooked through.

4.In the meantime, pour 1 cup (250ml) boiling water over the couscous in a tub. Cover and set aside for 5 minutes, then fluff with a fork and season with salt and pepper to taste.

5.Toss the seafood and soup into bowls, top with couscous and parsley, and garnish with lemon wedges.

SEAFOOD ESPETADA (PORTUGUESE SKEWERS)

Servings:4

INGREDIENTS

- 2 garlic cloves, finely chopped
- 2 long red chillies, seeds removed, finely chopped
- 2 tsp ground ginger
- 3 tsp sweet paprika
- 2 tsp dried oregano
- 1/3 cup (80ml) olive oil, plus extra to brush
- 4 limes, cut into wedges
- 24 prawns, peeled (tails intact), deveined
- 300g squid tubes, cut into 3cm strips
- 400g swordfish fillets, cut into 3cm pieces

- 4 corn cobs
- Flat-leaf parsley leaves, to serve

PREPARATION

1.Preheat a chargrill or a grill to high heat.

2.To make the marinade, combine the garlic, chili, ginger, paprika, oregano, and oil in a mixing bowl, and season with salt and pepper.

3.To make the skewers, thread 1 lime wedge, 1 prawn, 1 squid slice, and 1 swordfish piece onto a skewer and repeat. Rep with the rest of the skewers, then cover with the marinade.

4.Brush the corn with oil and chargrill it for 10 minutes, turning periodically, until blistered and soft.

5. Put it to the side. Brush the chargrill with oil and cook the skewers in batches for 2-3 minutes on each side, or until finished.

6.Slice the corn off the cob and serve with the skewers, garnished with parsley.

HOMESTYLE FISHCAKES WITH CAPER TARTARE

Servings:8

INGREDIENTS

- 250g smoked cod fillet
- 250g mashed potato (about 1 cup)
- 1 onion, grated
- 1 garlic clove, crushed
- 2 tbs salted capers, rinsed, plus 1 tbs extra to fry
- 2 tbs chopped flat-leaf parsley, plus 6 small sprigs to fry
- 2 hard-boiled eggs, finely chopped
- Pinch each of cayenne and nutmeg
- 2 tbs plain flour, seasoned

- 1 egg, beaten with 2 tbs milk
- 2 cups (140g) fresh breadcrumbs
- Sunflower oil, to shallow-fry
- CAPER TARTARE
- 2 tbs salted capers, rinsed
- 1 tbs cornichons (small pickled cucumbers), finely chopped
- 6 tarragon or parsley leaves, chopped
- 1 tsp Dijon mustard
- 2 tsp lemon juice, plus wedges to serve
- 1/2 cup (140ml) creme fraiche

PREPARATION

1.Place the fish in a frypan with enough water to cover it. Cook for 5 minutes over medium heat, or until the flesh easily flakes away. Drain the fish and flake the flesh, discarding the skin and bones. Combine potato, onion, garlic, capers, parsley, egg, and spices in a mixing bowl. Season with salt and pepper, then shape into 8 fishcakes.

2.In three shallow pans, combine the seasoned flour, beaten egg, and breadcrumbs. The fishcakes should be floured first, then dipped in egg, and finally coated in crumbs. To firm up, put on a plate and chill for 30 minutes.

3.To make the tartare, combine all of the ingredients in a mixing bowl and season with salt and pepper. Refrigerate until required.

4.In a fry pan, heat 3cm oil over medium-high heat. Extra capers and parsley sprigs should be fried separately for 30 seconds or until crisp, then drained on paper towels.

5.Cook the fishcakes in two batches for 2-3 minutes on each side until golden. Serve with tartare and lemon wedges, fried capers, and parsley on the side..

MACADAMIA-CRUSTED FISH WITH HERB SALAD

Servings:4

INGREDIENTS

- 2 cups (300g) unsalted macadamias
- 1 garlic clove, chopped
- Grated zest and juice of 1 lemon, plus wedges to serve
- 2 tablespoons extra virgin olive oil
- 1/2 bunch each flat-leaf parsley and chives
- 4 x 160g skinless barramundi fillets
- 50g mixed salad leaves, to serve

PREPARATION

1.Preheat the oven to 200°C and line a baking sheet with parchment paper.

2.In a small food processor, whiz the nuts, garlic, zest, half the juice, and 1 tablespoon oil into a coarse paste. Season and transfer to a cup. 2 tablespoons parsley, 2 tablespoons chives, finely chopped

3.Place the fish on the tray and top with the nut mixture. Bake for 15-20 minutes, or until the fish is opaque and the crust is golden.

4.Pick up the remaining parsley leaves and cut the chives in half. Combine salad leaves, remaining oil, and lemon juice in a mixing bowl. Season to taste, then serve with lemon wedges and fish.

PAN-FRIED KINGFISH WITH CABBAGE AND BACON

Servings:4

INGREDIENTS

- 25g unsalted butter
- 1/4 cup (60ml) olive oil
- 4 rashers bacon, chopped
- 1/4 cup (60ml) dry white wine
- 1 1/2 cups (375ml) chicken stock, heated
- 1/4 large savoy cabbage, finely shredded
- 2 thyme sprigs, plus extra to garnish
- 4 x 150g skinless kingfish fillets
- Mashed potato, to serve

PREPARATION

1.In a pan over medium-high heat, melt butter with 1 tablespoon oil. 5-6 minutes, stirring regularly, until bacon is softly golden. Simmer for 2-3 minutes after adding the wine and stock, then add the cabbage and thyme. Cook, covered, for 8-10 minutes, or until vegetables are tender. It's that time of year.

2.In a separate pan, heat the remaining 2 tablespoons of oil. Season the fish with salt and pepper and cook for 2-3 minutes on each side, or until cooked through. Serve with mashed potatoes and cabbage. Serve with thyme as a garnish.

YOGHURT-MARINATED FISH WRAPPED IN ZUCCHINI

Servings:4

INGREDIENTS

- 500g thick Greek-style yoghurt
- 1/2 bunch mint, leaves picked, roughly chopped
- 1 tsp dried chilli flakes
- Finely grated zest of 1 lemon and juice of 2 lemons, plus extra wedges to serve
- 4 x 200g skinless, firm white fish fillets (such as blue-eye)
- 2-3 long zucchinis, cut into 2mm-thick ribbons (a mandoline or vegetable peeler is ideal)

- 2 tbs olive oil
- Roughly chopped flat-leaf parsley, to serve

PREPARATION

1.In a small food processor cup, mix the yoghurt, mint, chilli flakes, lemon zest and juice, and whiz until smooth. It's that time of year.

2.In a shallow glass bowl, place the fish fillets. Half of the yoghurt marinade should be poured over the fish and spread with the back of a spoon. Refrigerate for 10 minutes after covering the dish with plastic wrap.

3.To soften zucchini slices, season with salt and set aside for 1-2 minutes.

4. Taking one of the fish fillets out of the marinade. Place 6-8 zucchini slices on top of the fish, slightly overlapping, and tuck the ends underneath. Rep with the remaining zucchini and fish fillets.

5.Preheat the oven to 200 degrees Celsius.

6.Cut four 30cm x 40cm baking paper rectangles. Fold one of the rectangles in half. One piece of fish should be put in the center along the crease when the bag is opened. Drizzle 1 tbsp olive oil over the fish and 1 tbsp marinade. It's that time of year. Fold the paper in half over the fish and trim the open edges into a semicircle with scissors. To close firmly, crimp at 1cm-2cm intervals, making firm creases. To secure the ends, twist them together and put them on a baking tray. Rep with the rest of the fish and paper.

7.Cook for 8-10 minutes, or until golden and puffed. Enable the parcels to rest for 2-3 minutes after removing the tray from the oven.

8.Assemble the parcels on serving plates. Carefully cut the fish open with scissors, then sprinkle with parsley and serve with lemon wedges.

MINI FISH PIES

Servings:4

INGREDIENTS

- 1 cup (250ml) white wine
- 1 tbs finely chopped dill, stalks reserved
- 1 tbs finely chopped tarragon, stalks reserved
- 1 tbs finely chopped flat-leaf parsley, stalks reserved
- 1 leek, thinly sliced
- 3 eschalots, thinly sliced
- 250g skinless salmon fillet, cut into 4cm pieces.
- 250g green prawns, peeled, deveined
- 8 scallops, roe removed, halved
- 25g plain flour

- 250g unsalted butter, softened
- 300ml pure (thin) cream
- 1kg King Edward potatoes, peeled, chopped
- 100ml milk
- 2 egg yolks
- Salad leaves, to serve

PREPARATION

1.Preheat the oven to 180 degrees Celsius.

2.In a large frypan over medium heat, mix the wine and 1 cup (250ml) water. 1 teaspoon coarsely ground black pepper, herb stalks, leek, and eschalot Bring to a low boil, then reduce to a low heat and cook for 2 minutes, or until the flavors have infused.

3.Add the salmon and cook for 2 minutes, turning halfway through. Cook for another minute, or until the prawns and scallops are just starting to change color. Using a slotted spoon, remove the seafood and put it in a clean cup. Delete from the equation.

4.Combine flour and 25g butter in a small cup. Return the stock to medium-low heat after removing the herb stalks from the pan. Bring to a low simmer, then add 1 tablespoon of the butter mixture at a time, whisking to combine with each addition. Season with salt and pepper and cook, stirring constantly, for 3 minutes, or until the sauce has thickened. Cook for another 2 minutes after adding the milk. Allow time for cooling.

5.In a large saucepan of cold, salted water, position the potato. Bring to a boil, then reduce to a low heat and cook for 12-15 minutes, or until the potatoes are tender. Drain and run through a potato ricer or mash with a potato masher until smooth. Mix in the remaining 225g butter while the potato is still sweet. Season with salt and pepper and set aside the milk and egg yolks.

6.In a 350ml ovenproof dish, fold the seafood and chopped herbs into the cooled sauce. Cook for 15-20 minutes, until the potato is bubbling and golden. Remove the dish from the oven and top with salad leaves..

SCALLOP AND PRESERVED LEMON SQUID INK LINGUINI

Servings:2

INGREDIENTS

- 200g squid-ink or regular linguini
- 2 tbs olive oil
- 10 scallops, roe removed
- 2 garlic cloves, thinly sliced
- 1 long red chilli, seeds removed, thinly sliced
- 1 cup (250ml) dry white wine
- 20g unsalted butter
- 1/4 preserved lemon, pith and flesh removed, rind thinly sliced

PREPARATION

1.Cook the pasta according to the package directions in a wide saucepan of lightly salted boiling water. Drain the water.

2.In a wide frypan, heat 1 tablespoon oil over high heat. Season scallops with salt and pepper, then cook for 1 minute on each side, or until golden brown and cooked through. Remove the object and set it aside. 1 tablespoon oil remaining in pan, then cook garlic and chilli, stirring constantly, for 1 minute or until golden. Increase the heat to high and cook for 5 minutes, or until the liquid has evaporated. Remove the pan from the heat and stir in the rind.

3.Return the frypan to medium heat and add the pasta. Stir in the scallops after gently tossing to mix. Season to taste and serve..

SAUTEED SCALLOPS WITH JALAPEÑO DRESSING

Servings:4

INGREDIENTS

- 1 fresh jalapeño chilli, seeds removed, finely chopped
- 1/2 small red onion, finely chopped
- 1 tbs grapeseed oil
- 1 tsp extra virgin olive oil
- 1/4 cup (60ml) lemon or lime juice
- 12 scallops on the half-shell,orange roe removed
- 2 tbs olive oil
- 10g unsalted butter

- JALAPEÑO DRESSING (MAKES 100ML)
- 4 small (50g) jalapeño chillies, seeds removed, roughly chopped
- 1 small garlic clove, chopped
- 2 1/2 tbs (50ml) rice vinegar
- 2 1/2 tbs (50ml) olive oil

PREPARATION

1.In a mixing bowl, combine the jalapeo, onion, grapeseed oil, extra virgin olive oil, lemon juice, and 1/2 teaspoon salt. Set aside the jalapeo salsa.

2.To make the jalapeo dressing, puree the jalapeo, garlic, vinegar, and 1 1/2 teaspoons salt in a stick blender until smooth. Gradually incorporate the olive oil into the mixture, then strain through a sieve. Set aside the dressing.

3.Take the scallops out of the shells and set them aside. Scallop shells should be cleaned and dried with a paper towel.

4.In a broad frypan, heat the oil over high heat. Using salt and pepper, season the scallops. Cook the scallops for 1 1/2 minutes on each hand, or until golden and translucent in the middle. To glaze the scallops, apply the butter for the last 30 seconds of cooking.

5.To serve, divide the jalapeo dressing among the scallop shells, top each with a scallop, and finish with the salsa..

SCALLOP AND SILKEN TOFU WITH SOY AND WASABI BUTTER

Servings:4

INGREDIENTS

- 8 scallops in the half shell, roe removed
- 300g silken firm tofu, drained
- 100g unsalted butter
- 3 garlic cloves, finely chopped
- 1 tsp wasabi paste
- 1 tsp caster sugar
- 2 tbs soy sauce
- 1 punnet mustard cress

PREPARATION

1.Preheat the oven to 160 degrees Celsius. Scallops and tofu should be cut into small, equal-sized cubes. Scallop shells should be put on a 2. In a saucepan, melt the butter over medium-high heat for 2 1/2 minutes, or until browned. Remove from the heat and set aside to cool slightly. Whisk together the garlic, wasabi, sugar, and soy sauce.

3.Preheat oven to 400°F for 4 minutes, or until scallops and tofu are warm. To eat, drizzle with sauce and top with mustard cress..

MATT MORAN'S GRILLED HERVEY BAY SCALLOPS WITH TOGARASHI & CHILLI SYRUP

Servings:4

INGREDIENTS

- 1/2 tsp cornflour
- 1/4 cup (55g) caster sugar
- 1 long red chilli, seeds removed, finely chopped
- 1/3 cup (80ml) rice vinegar
- 1 tsp grated ginger

- 2 pinches of shichimi togarashi (Japanese spice mix of salt, chilli, black pepper, sesame seeds, dried orange peel, poppyseeds and nori)
- 16 Hervey Bay scallops, roe removed
- 1 tbs olive oil
- Micro cress, to serve

PREPARATION

1.In a mixing bowl, combine the cornflour and 2 tsp cold water. Delete from the equation.

2.In a small saucepan over medium heat, combine the sugar, chili, and 2 tablespoons water. Bring to a boil, then reduce to a low heat and cook for 1 minute. Cook for 1 minute more, or until slightly thickened, after adding the cornflour mixture. Take the pan off the heat and whisk in the vinegar, ginger, and togarashi. Enable to cool before serving.

3.In a broad frypan, heat the oil over high heat. Season scallops with salt and pepper after tossing them in the oil. Sear scallops in batches for 30 seconds on each side, or until caramelized but opaque in the middle.

4.Serve by drizzling togarashi and chilli syrup dressing over scallops and scattering micro cress on top..

SEARED SCALLOPS WITH CREME FRAICHE AND WASABI CRUNCH

Servings:4

INGREDIENTS

- 1/4 cup (60g) creme fraiche
- 1 tbs finely chopped chives
- 1 tbs finely chopped dill
- Finely grated zest of 1 lime
- 2 tsp rice vinegar
- 2 tbs peanut or sunflower oil, plus extra to brush
- 2 tbs tamari
- 20 scallops, roe removed
- 1/4 cup (25g) wasabi peas, lightly crushed

- Micro herbs, to serve

PREPARATION

1.Combine the creme fraiche, chives, dill, lime zest, and rice vinegar in a mixing bowl. Season with salt and pepper and set aside.

2.Combine the oil and tamari in a mixing bowl. Delete from the equation. Preheat a skillet over high heat. Season scallops with salt and pepper after brushing them with oil. Cook scallops in batches for 30 seconds on each side or until golden but still translucent in the middle.

3.To serve, put a dollop of creme fraiche on each serving plate and top with scallops. Drizzle with tamari dressing, then add wasabi peas and micro herbs to finish..

SCALLOP TARTARE

S

Servings:4

INGREDIENTS

- Finely grated zest of 1/2 lemon
- 1 tbs rice wine vinegar
- 2 tsp soy sauce
- 1 tsp each fish sauce and sesame oil
- 2 tbs sunflower oil
- 8 large scallops, thinly sliced horizontally
- Finely grated zest of 1 lime
- Mixed herbs, to serve

PREPARATION

1.Preheat the oven to 100 degrees Celsius. On a baking tray, scatter the zest and 1 tbsp sea salt, then roast for 12-15 minutes, stirring 2-3 times, until dry. To render a coarse powder, move to a mortar and pestle.

2.In a mixing bowl, combine the vinegar, soy sauce, fish sauce, and oils. Delete from the equation.

3.Assemble the scallops on the bowls. Drizzle with soy dressing after applying lime zest and a pinch of lemon sea salt. Sprinkle with spices, season with salt and pepper, and serve.

TEQUILA-SPIKED SCALLOP CEVICHE

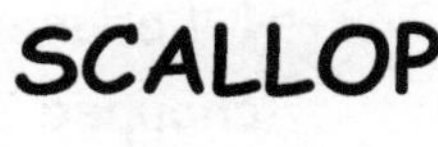

Servings:4

INGREDIENTS

- 1/4 baguette, thinly sliced
- 1/4 cup (60ml) extra virgin olive oil, plus extra to brush
- 12 large scallops, roe removed, cut into 1cm pieces
- 1/4 cup (60ml) tequila
- 1/4 cup (60ml) lime juice
- 1/2 red onion, finely chopped
- 1 tomato, seeds removed, roughly chopped
- 1 long red chilli, seeds removed, finely chopped

- 1 Lebanese cucumber, seeds removed, roughly chopped
- 1/2 bunch coriander, leaves roughly chopped

PREPARATION

1.Preheat the oven to 170 degrees Celsius. Brush the baguette slices with oil, then place them on a baking tray and bake until golden and crisp, about 10-12 minutes. Enable to cool before serving.

2.In the meantime, toss the scallops in a bowl with the tequila and lime juice. Enable 10 minutes for the lime juice's acid to 'warm' the scallops. Drain the liquid, reserving 2 teaspoons.

3.In a mixing bowl, gently toss the scallops, reserved sauce, onion, tomato, chili, cucumber, coriander, and remaining 1/4 cup (60ml) olive oil to blend. With the toasts, serve.

TEQUILA SCALLOP CEVICHE

S

Servings:4

INGREDIENTS

- Juice of 4 limes
- 1 long green chilli, seeds removed, finely chopped
- 1 teaspoon fish sauce
- 2 1/2 tablespoons brown sugar
- 1 Lebanese cucumber, seeds removed, finely chopped
- 2 tablespoons tequila
- 16 scallops, roe removed, thinly sliced into thin discs
- 2 eschalots, finely chopped
- 2 tomatoes, seeds removed, finely chopped

- 1/2 avocado, finely chopped
- Micro coriander or micro cress (see notes), to serve

PREPARATION

1.In a food processor, whiz lime juice, chili, fish sauce, sugar, one-quarter of the cucumber, and 1 teaspoon salt until smooth. Season with salt and pepper after whizzing in the tequila. Cover and chill for 30 minutes for the flavors to infuse, then move to a non-reactive bowl with the scallop and eschalot.

2.Assemble the ceviche on serving plates. Serve with the remaining cucumber, onion, avocado, and micro herbs on top.

CARAMELISED SCALLOP MIANG (BETEL LEAVES)

Servings:20

INGREDIENTS

- 2/3 cup (50g) shredded coconut, toasted
- 1/2 cup (75g) roasted peanuts, crushed
- 2 tablespoons chilli bean paste or chilli jam (see notes)
- 1 1/2 tablespoons fish sauce
- 2 tablespoons palm sugar or brown sugar
- 1/4 cup (75g) sweet chilli sauce
- 2 tablespoons lime juice
- Peanut oil or rice bran oil, to brush

- 20 scallops, roe removed
- 20 betel leaves (see notes)
- Fried Asian shallots (see notes), coriander leaves and finely shredded kaffir lime leaves, to serve

PREPARATION

1.Miang Caramelized Scallops (betel leaves). Panna cotta with lime and coconut on the right.

2.Heat a broad frypan over medium-high heat and brush with a little oil. Season the scallops with salt and cook in batches for 30 seconds on each side, or until golden and caramelized on the outside but still opaque in the center - add a little more oil if necessary.

3.Place 1 heaping teaspoon of chilli sauce on each betel leaf, top with a scallop, and finish with fried Asian shallots, coriander, and a kaffir lime leaf. Serve right away.

SCALLOP TARTS WITH CARROT AND CARDAMOM PUREE

Servings:24

INGREDIENTS

- 3 carrots, chopped
- 1/3 cup (80ml) fresh orange juice
- Pinch of saffron threads
- 6 cardamom pods, lightly bruised
- 50g unsalted butter
- 100g thick Greek-style yoghurt
- Zest and juice of 1 lemon

- 1/4 cup each sesame and nigella seeds
- 2 tablespoons ghee
- 24 scallops (without roe)
- 24 x 4cm pre-baked tart shells
- Coriander sprigs, to garnish

PREPARATION

1.In a saucepan, mix the carrots, orange juice, saffron, and cardamom with enough water to cover. Bring to a boil, then reduce to a low heat and continue to cook for another 25-30 minutes, or until carrots are tender. Cardamom pods should be drained and discarded. Allow carrots to cool slightly before combining with butter, salt, and pepper in a food processor. Return to the pan after whizzing to form a smooth puree. Keep yourself wet.

2.In a small mixing bowl, add the yoghurt and lemon juice. Season with salt and pepper to taste, then chill until needed.

3.In a mixing bowl, combine the seeds. Delete from the equation.

4.In a pan over medium-high heat, melt the ghee. Season scallops on both sides with salt and pepper, then cook in batches for 30 seconds on each side, or until they begin to change color. In a large mixing bowl, toss the warm scallops with the seed mixture.

5.Pour a heaping teaspoon of puree into each tart shell, top with a scallop and a drizzle of yoghurt dressing, and finish with coriander sprigs and zest.

SEARED SCALLOPS WITH BACON DUST AND CRUSHED AVOCADO ON TOAST

Servings:4

INGREDIENTS

- 3 bacon rashers
- 1 teaspoon coriander seeds, toasted
- 2 long red chillies, seeds removed
- 2 avocados
- 1/4 red onion, finely chopped
- 1 tomato, seeds removed, chopped
- 1/2 bunch coriander, leaves chopped
- 1 tablespoon lime juice, plus wedges to serve
- 1 tablespoon olive oil

- 12 scallops without roe
- 4 slices sourdough bread, toasted
- Micro herbs or small coriander leaves, to serve

PREPARATION

1.Preheat the oven to 190°C and line a baking sheet with parchment paper. Place bacon on a baking sheet and bake for 15-20 minutes, or until crisp and dry. Enable to cool on a plate lined with paper towels. In a small processor, mix the bacon and coriander seeds and process until finely ground (alternatively, chop very finely).

2.Thinly slice 1 chilli and set aside for garnish, then finely chop the remaining chilli and combine with avocado, onion, tomato, coriander leaves, and lime juice in a mortar or big mixing bowl. Using a pestle or a fork, mash until a coarse paste develops.

3.In a large skillet, heat the oil over high heat. Cook for 30 seconds on each side or until just opaque, seasoning scallops as required. Toast the bread and spread the avocado mixture on it. 3 scallops on top of each, followed by the bacon dust, sliced chilli, and herbs. And lime wedges on the side.

CARAMELISED SCALLOPS WITH BEETROOT, WALNUTS

Servings:4

INGREDIENTS

- 1 bunch baby beetroot, scrubbed
- 1 green apple, quartered, cored
- 2 red witlof (Belgian endive), leaves separated
- 100g wild rocket leaves
- 8-12 scallops, cleaned
- 1 tablespoon olive oil
- 2 tablespoons roughly chopped walnuts, toasted
- DRESSING
- 1/4 cup (60ml) olive oil or walnut oil (see Notes)

- 2 tablespoons red wine vinegar
- 1 tablespoon honey
- 1 teaspoon Dijon mustard

PREPARATION

1.Preheat the oven to 180 degrees Celsius.

2.Place the beetroot on a large sheet of foil and fold it in half to make a parcel. Roast for 1 hour, or until beets are soft. After the beetroot has cooled, peel it and cut it into wedges.

3.To make the dressing, whisk together the olive or walnut oil, vinegar, honey, and mustard in a mixing bowl, season with salt and pepper, and thin with a splash of water. Thinly slice the apple and toss it with the witlof and rocket in the dressing. Set aside as you finish preparing the scallops.

4.In a dry frypan, heat the oil over medium heat. Season scallops with sea salt and freshly ground black pepper after brushing them with oil. Sear scallops in batches for 30 seconds on each side, or until caramelized on the outside but opaque in the middle.

5.Toss the salad between plates, then add the scallops, beets, and walnuts. Drizzle with any remaining dressing and serve..

SEARED SCALLOPS WITH CHORIZO AND ROAST

Servings:8

INGREDIENTS

- 3 red capsicums
- 2 vine-ripened tomatoes
- 1/2 cup (125ml) olive oil
- 4 eschalots, finely chopped
- 4 garlic cloves, finely chopped
- 2 chorizos (about 250g), peeled, finely chopped
- 2 tbs chopped flat-leaf parsley

- 16 large scallops on the half shell, orange roe removed
- 1/2 tsp smoked paprika (pimenton)

PREPARATION

Preheat the oven to 200 degrees Celsius. Roast for 25-30 minutes, rotating once, until the skins are charred and the flesh is soft, on a baking tray. Remove from the oven and place in a plastic bag to cool. Cut a small cross in the base of each tomato in the meantime. Blanch for 20 seconds in a large saucepan of boiling water, then plunge into ice water for 30 seconds. Remove the seeds and finely cut the flesh after peeling. Delete from the equation.

Break the capsicums over a bowl until they've cooled enough to handle to catch all of the juices. Remove and discard the skin and seeds, then finely chop the remaining ingredients. Put aside the chopped capsicum in the mixing bowl.

5.In a medium-sized frypan, heat 100ml olive oil. Cook, stirring regularly, for 5 minutes, or until the eschalots and garlic are soft and the chorizo is browned, until the eschalots and garlic are soft and the chorizo is browned. Simmer for 3-5 minutes, until some of the excess moisture has evaporated and the sauce is thick but not dry, after which add the tomatoes and capsicum mixture. Season with salt and pepper after adding the chopped parsley. While you're waiting for the scallops to cook, keep them warm.

6.Set the scallops aside after separating them from their shells. Put aside after washing the shells and patting them dry with a paper towel.

7.In a large nonstick frypan, heat 2 teaspoons oil over high heat. Season the scallops with salt and pepper on both sides. Cook the scallops for 1 minute on each hand, or until golden but still translucent in the middle, in two batches. Using the remaining oil and scallops, repeat the process.

8.Toss the scallops on top of the chorizo and capsicum sauce and split among the shells. Serve right away..

SCALLOPS WITH BREADCRUMBS, PEAS AND

Servings:6

INGREDIENTS

- 2 tablespoons chopped flat-leaf parsley
- 2 garlic cloves, finely chopped
- 4 slices prosciutto, chopped
- Pinch of chilli flakes
- 1 cup (70g) sourdough breadcrumbs
- 1/4 cup (60ml) extra virgin olive oil
- 24 scallops on the half shell, roe removed
- 2 cups (240g) frozen peas
- 1/2 cup (40g) finely grated parmesan

- 2 tablespoons dry white wine

PREPARATION

1.Pulse parsley, garlic, prosciutto, chili, and breadcrumbs together in a mini processor. Season with salt and pepper, then pulse until just mixed. Place scallops on a baking sheet in their shells.

2.Set the grill to medium-high heat.

3. Blanch peas for 2 minutes in salted boiling water. Drain the water. Season and toss with parmesan cheese. Keep yourself wet.

4.Drizzle wine over scallops and grill for 1-2 minutes, or until crumbs are golden and scallops are only fried. Serve on a platter with parmesan peas scattered on top.

SCALLOPS WITH FRESH MANGO AND SAFFRON SAUCE

Servings:6

INGREDIENTS

- 2 ripe mangoes
- 2 Lebanese cucumbers
- 1 lime, juiced
- 5ml (1 teaspoon) white wine vinegar
- 40ml (2 tablespoons) olive oil, plus extra to brush
- 1 tablespoon chopped fresh coriander
- 300ml white wine
- 300ml thickened cream
- 1 teaspoon saffron threads

- 36 large scallops with roe, cleaned

PREPARATION

1.Slice the flesh of the mangoes into long slivers after peeling them. Delete from the equation.

2.Cucumber slices can be thinly sliced using a vegetable peeler. Combine the lime juice, vinegar, oil, and coriander in a mixing bowl.

3.In a small saucepan, combine the wine, milk, and saffron and cook for 5-6 minutes, or until thickened. Delete from the equation.

4.Place three scallops on each skewer and drizzle with olive oil. Salt and pepper to taste. Cook the scallops for 1 minute on each side in a nonstick frying pan over high heat until opaque. Serve with saffron cream and two skewers of mango and cucumber on each plate.

STEAMED SCALLOPS WITH CHINESE PICKLED

Servings:6

INGREDIENTS

- 1/2 teaspoon sesame oil
- 1 tablespoon peanut oil
- 1 tablespoon grated ginger
- 2 garlic cloves, finely chopped
- 1 small red chilli, seeds removed, finely chopped
- 1/3 cup (80ml) soy sauce
- 24 scallops in the half shell
- Coriander leaves, to serve

CHINESE PICKLED VEGETABLES

- 100ml rice vinegar
- 2 tablespoons caster sugar
- 1/2 red onion, thinly sliced
- 1 carrot, cut into matchsticks
- 1/2 Lebanese cucumber, seeds removed, cut into matchsticks

PREPARATION

1.To prepare the vegetables, mix vinegar and sugar in a pan. Bring to a boil, stirring constantly to melt the sugar. Reduce the heat to low and continue to cook for another 2 minutes. Remove from heat and set aside to cool after adding the vegetables.

2.Heat the oils in a wok over high heat, then add the ginger, garlic, and chili pepper and stir-fry for a few seconds. Remove the chicken and put it in a bowl with 1/4 cup (60ml) water and soy sauce.

3.In 2 wide bamboo steamers, arrange scallops in a single sheet. Top with sauce, then stack steamers, cover, and steam for 5 minutes or until just cooked over a wok or large pan of simmering water.

4.Top each plate with four scallops, vegetables, and coriander.

VEAL SCALLOPINE WITH FENNEL AND PARMESAN SALAD

Servings:4

INGREDIENTS

- 4 x 150g veal schnitzels
- 1 1/2 cups (225g) plain flour, seasoned
- 3 cups (210g) day-old fine breadcrumbs
- 2 tablespoons finely chopped flat-leaf parsley
- 1 cup (80g) finely grated parmesan
- 2 eggs, beaten with 1 tablespoon Dijon mustard
- Light olive oil, to shallow-fry

- Lemon wedges and potato mashed with
- Grated parmesan, to serve
- FENNEL AND PARMESAN SALAD
- 1 red onion, thinly sliced
- 1/4 cup (60ml) olive oil
- 2 tablespoons lemon juice
- 1 fennel bulb (or 2 small), thinly sliced
- 2 cups flat-leaf parsley leaves
- 60g parmesan, shaved
- 1 cup shredded radicchio leaves

PREPARATION

1.To make the salad, put the onion in a small bowl and cover with boiling water for 5 minutes. Drain and set aside to cool. Season with salt and pepper, then toss with the onion and the rest of the salad ingredients. Delete from the equation.

2.Place the veal between two sheets of plastic wrap and roll it out gently. On a pan, spread flour. On a separate pan, combine the crumbs, parsley, and parmesan. The veal is floured first, then dipped in egg, then crumbs. In a medium-high-heat frypan, heat the oil. Cook the veal in batches for 2-3 minutes on each hand, or until golden brown. Using a paper towel, absorb excess liquid. Keep warm as you finish the rest of the meal. Serve with lettuce, lemon mash, and parmesan cheese..

SCALLOPS WITH PEPERONATA AND AIOLI

Servings:4

INGREDIENTS

- 290g jar peperonata
- 2 tablespoons Ardmona Pureed Tomatoes
- 20 scallops without roe
- 2 tablespoons olive oil
- 50g mixed baby salad leaves (mesclun)
- Extra virgin olive oil, to drizzle
- 200g jar aioli (garlic mayonnaise)

PREPARATION

1.In a saucepan, heat the peperonata and passata over low heat for 2-3 minutes, or until heated through. Season with freshly ground black pepper and sea salt.

2.Brush both sides of the scallops with oil and season with salt and pepper. Cook the scallops in batches in a wide frypan over high heat for 30 seconds per side until golden brown but still translucent in the middle.

3.Assemble the peperonata, scallops, and salad leaves on individual serving plates. Season with salt and pepper, then drizzle with extra virgin olive oil and aioli before serving.

SCALLOPS, JERUSALEM ARTICHOKES AND RADICCHIO

Servings:4

INGREDIENTS

- 24 fresh scallops, roe attached
- 8 Jerusalem artichokes
- Zest and juice of 1 lemon
- 100g unsalted butter
- 2 tablespoons extra virgin olive oil
- Sea salt
- 1/2 cup (125ml) verjuice
- 2 tablespoons freshly chopped flat-leaf parsley
- 2-3 small radicchio leaves per person, to serve

PREPARATION

1.Scallops should be washed by scraping the digestive tract but not the roe. Artichokes should be peeled and thinly sliced lengthwise. To avoid discoloration, apply a splash of lemon juice. Artichokes that aren't wet.

2.In a nonstick pan, melt half the butter and half the oil over medium-high heat until nut brown. Fry the artichokes until golden (in batches if necessary). Place the chicken on a plate and set it aside.

3. Season scallops with lemon zest, salt, and black pepper. Over medium-high heat, melt the remaining butter and oil in the pan, and sear the scallops in two batches (as they must not poach) until golden on one side, then flip to cook the other side.

4.Use verjuice to deglaze the last pan of scallops. Toss the scallops, artichokes, and parsley together. Season to taste, and if possible, add a little more lemon juice and oil. In radicchio leaves, serve.

SCALLOPS WITH BLACK BEANS AND CHILLI

Servings:4

INGREDIENTS

- 3 tablespoons Chinese salted black beans, rinsed
- 2cm piece fresh ginger, peeled, cut into very thin matchsticks
- 1 teaspoon sugar
- 1 tablespoon Chinese rice wine (shaohsing) or dry sherry
- 3 tablespoons (1/4 cup) soy sauce
- 1 teaspoon sesame oil
- 8 fresh sea scallops on the shell

- 1 long red chilli, seeds removed, very finely sliced lengthways

PREPARATION

1.Soak beans in cold water for about 5 minutes after each update. Half of the beans should be drained and gently crushed.

2.Combine the beans, ginger, sugar, rice wine, soy sauce, and sesame oil in a mixing bowl. Pour the sauce over the scallops and top with the chilli.

3.Steam the scallops for 4-5 minutes, or until just cooked, in a steamer over simmering water. Serve immediately.

WARM SALAD OF SCALLOPS AND WALNUTS

Servings:6

INGREDIENTS

- 5 slices of good-quality bread
- 1/2 cup (125ml) olive oil, plus 1-2 tablespoons extra for croutons
- 24 scallops, roe removed
- 1 tablespoon walnut oil
- 2 tablespoons sherry vinegar
- 100g baby salad leaves (mesclun)
- 1 radicchio, outer leaves discarded
- 1 cup walnuts, toasted, chopped

PREPARATION

1.Cut the bread into very small cubes for the croutons. In a pan over medium heat, heat the extra olive oil and fry, rotating to ensure even cooking, for 3-4 minutes, or until golden.

2.Set aside on a paper towel to drain.

3.Using a paper towel, pat the scallops dry and season with salt and pepper.

4.To make the dressing, whisk together 1/3 cup (80ml) olive oil, walnut oil, and sherry vinegar, then season to taste.

5.Toss the salad leaves, radicchio, and walnuts with the croutons in a dish.

6.Heat the remaining oil in a frypan over high heat and cook the scallops when it is very hot (you may need to do this in batches). Cook for 30 seconds on either hand, or until golden on the outside and opaque in the middle.

7.Place the salad on serving plates after tossing it with the dressing. Place 4 scallops on each plate and serve right away..

SCALLOPS WITH SPICY RICE

Servings:4

INGREDIENTS

- 12 large scallops without roe
- 2 tsp mild curry powder
- 1/2 tsp brown sugar
- 1 tbs vegetable oil
- 1 cup basmati rice
- 1 tsp ground turmeric
- 1 cup frozen peas
- 1 red chilli, seeds removed, sliced
- 2 tbs cashews, lightly toasted
- Watercress, to garnish (optional)

PREPARATION

1.Coat the scallops in the curry powder, brown sugar, and half of the vegetable oil in a plastic container. Place in the refrigerator until ready to use.

2.In a pan of boiling salted water, combine the basmati rice and turmeric. Cook, stirring occasionally, for 8 minutes over medium-low heat, or until the rice is almost finished. Cook for another minute after adding the peas. Return the mixture to the pan after draining. Set back, protected.

3.Brush the remaining vegetable oil into a non-stick frypan and position it over high heat. Cook the scallops for 1 minute on each side when the pan is heated. Place the rice on serving plates and top with the cashews after stirring in the sliced chilli. Serve with the scallops and, if desired, watercress leaves..

CHILLI JAM SCALLOPS WITH ASIAN GREENS

Servings:4

INGREDIENTS

- 2 bunches Chinese broccoli (gai lan), trimmed, cut into 6cm lengths
- 20 scallops without roe
- 1 1/2 tablespoons chilli jam*
- 2 teaspoons olive oil
- 1 small onion, thinly sliced
- 2 teaspoons light soy sauce

PREPARATION

1.Steam the Chinese broccoli for 2-3 minutes, covered, in a large saucepan of boiling water until just tender. Drain the water and set it aside.

2.Toss the scallops with 1 tablespoon of the chilli jam in the meantime. 1 teaspoon olive oil 1 teaspoon olive oil 1 teaspoon When the pan is heated, add the scallops and cook for 1 minute on each hand, or until they are just done. Remove the skillet from the heat and cover to stay warm.

3.Reduce the heat to medium and apply the remaining teaspoon of oil to the pan. Cook for 3-4 minutes, or until onion is softened. Toss in the remaining 1/2 tablespoon chilli jam and the broccoli to cover. Remove from the heat and apply the soy sauce.

4. Place the vegetables in bowls and top with scallops.

SCALLOPS WITH NOODLES AND OYSTER SAUCE

Servings:4

INGREDIENTS

- 200g packet egg noodles
- 2 tablespoons peanut oil
- 1 bunch broccolini, halved into florets and stems
- 24 scallops (without roe)
- 2 teaspoons sesame oil
- 2 tablespoons oyster sauce, plus extra to drizzle
- 1 teaspoon soy sauce
- 1 teaspoon sugar
- 1 long red chilli, seeds removed, thinly sliced

- 1/2 bunch spring onions, thinly sliced on the diagonal
- 1 bunch coriander, leaves picked

PREPARATION

Cook the noodles as directed on the package, then drain and toss with 1 teaspoon peanut oil.

In a saucepan of boiling salted water, blanch the broccolini for 1 minute. Drain and rinse under cold running water.

Clean the scallops with a paper towel before brushing them with sesame oil. In a large nonstick frypan, heat the remaining peanut oil over medium-high heat. When the pan is warmed, add the scallops in 6 batches. Cook for 1 minute on each hand, or until sear marks appear but the center remains opaque. Place on a plate to cool.

Stir together the oyster sauce, soy sauce, sugar, and 2 tablespoons of water in the frypan. Return the scallops, noodles, and broccolini to the pan and toss quickly to heat through. Combine the chilli, spring onion, and coriander in a mixing bowl. Serve immediately with extra oyster sauce drizzled on top.

SALMON AND SCALLOP CEVICHE

SERVINGS:6

INGREDIENTS

- 400g salmon fillet, pin-boned
- 300g scallops, roe removed
- 1 cup (250ml) fresh lime juice
- 4 vine-ripened tomatoes, chopped
- 3 long green chilies, seeds removed, finely chopped
- 6 spring onions, finely chopped
- 1/3 cup chopped coriander leaves, plus extra to garnish

- 1/2 telegraph cucumber, peeled, chopped
- 1 avocado, flesh chopped
- 1/4 cup (60ml) olive oil
- Baby cos lettuce leaves (1-2 per person, depending on size), to serve

PREPARATION

. Cut the seafood into small cubes and toss it in a bowl of lime juice. Refrigerate for 4 hours, sealed. Drain the juice and season with sea salt and pepper before adding the tomato, chili, spring onion, coriander, cucumber, avocado, and oil.

To eat, layer the ceviche on top of the lettuce leaves on bowls. Serve immediately, garnished with extra coriander leaves and lime wedges if desired.

CONCLUSION

PROVIDES OMEGA-3 FATTY ACIDS

One of the main reasons fish is so good for us is because it contains high levels of omega-3 fatty acids. In a world where most people consume far too many omega-6 fatty acids from refined vegetable oils, salad dressings, and processed spices, increasing omega-3 foods is urgently needed.

Omega-3 fatty acids act as a counterbalance to omega-6 fats and help keep inflammation down by balancing the levels of omega-3 and omega-6 fatty acids. Omega-3 fatty acids are considered to be anti-inflammatory, while omega-6 fatty acids are anti-inflammatory. We need both types, but many people lack omega-3 fatty acids. Consuming higher omega-3 levels has been linked to better mental health, lower triglyceride levels, improved reproductive health and fertility, better hormone control, and a lower risk of diabetes.

HELPS IN LOWERING INFLAMMATION

The reason the omega-3s found in fish are so valuable is mainly because of their ability to fight inflammation. They help control inflammatory diseases that lead to numerous diseases, including cancer, rheumatoid arthritis, and asthma.

Both types of polyunsaturated fats described above play an important role in the body and contribute to the formation of our hormones, cell membranes and immune

responses. But omega-3 and omega-6 fatty acids have opposite effects when it comes to inflammation. In general, too much omega-6 and too little omega-3 cause inflammation. Inflammation is believed to contribute to the development of chronic conditions like cancer, diabetes, heart disease, and more.

PROMOTES HEART HEALTH

EPA and DHA are two omega-3 fatty acids that are essential for controlling inflammation and promoting heart health. Studies show that daily consumption of EPA and DHA can help reduce the risk of heart disease and death from heart disease, sometimes as effective as prescription drugs like statins. The combination of nutrients in seafood also helps regulate the heartbeat, lower blood pressure and cholesterol, reduce blood clot formation, and lower triglycerides. All of these can help protect against heart disease and stroke.

CAN HELP PROTECT AGAINST CANCER

Research shows that eating more fish and seafood high in omega-3s benefits the immune system and helps fight cancer by suppressing inflammation. While a vegetarian diet has been linked to a lower incidence of certain types of cancer (such as colon cancer), pescatarianism is associated with an even lower risk compared to vegetarians and non-vegetarians, according to some studies.

Several studies also suggest that consuming plenty of omega-3 fatty acids may help those previously diagnosed with cancer by stopping tumor growth. A pescatarian lifestyle high in omega-3s can also help people undergoing chemotherapy or other cancer treatments, as they help maintain muscle mass and regulate inflammatory responses that are already compromised in cancer patients.

COMBATS COGNITIVE DECLINE

Omega-3 fatty acids like DHA are vital for proper brain development and maintenance of cognitive function in old age. Many studies have shown that low omega-3 levels in the elderly are linked to several markers of impaired brain function, including dementia or Alzheimer's disease. Lower omega-3 levels during pregnancy have even been linked to children who have lower memory test scores and learning difficulties.

BOOSTS THE MOOD

Because they fight oxidative stress, which affects the proper functioning of the brain, the omega-3s from fish and seafood have been linked to better mental health and a lower risk of dementia, depression, anxiety, and ADHD. This means that a Pescatarian diet can be a natural anti-anxiety remedy and help manage the symptoms of ADHD while fighting off symptoms of depression.

SUPPORTS WEIGHT LOSS

Many people have started using the Pescatarian diet for weight loss, and for good reason. Low intake of omega-3

fatty acids has been linked to obesity and weight gain. Studies also show that people who eat more plant-based foods (including vegetarians) tend to have lower BMIs and better weight management, probably because they eat more fiber and fewer calories.

Not only that, but healthy proteins and fats are critical to feeling full, and many of the nutrients found in fish can help reduce cravings. Regardless of your diet, aim for a high intake of fruits, vegetables, high quality proteins, healthy fats, seeds, nuts, fiber, and phytochemicals. All of these can help you lose weight quickly and keep it off.

PESCATARIAN DIET RECIPES FOR BEGINNERS

+50 Delicious Simple Seafood Recipes

Arthur Foster

Disclaimer

The information contained i is meant to serve as a comprehensive collection of strategies that the author of this eBook has done research about. Summaries, strategies, tips and tricks are only recommendation by the author, and reading this eBook will not guarantee that one's results will exactly mirror the author's results. The author of the eBook has made all reasonable effort to provide current and accurate information for the readers of the eBook. The author and it's associates will not be held liable for any unintentional error or omissions that may be found. The material in the eBook may include information by third parties. Third party materials comprise of opinions expressed by their owners. As such, the author of the eBook does not assume responsibility or liability for any third party material or opinions. Whether because of the progression of the internet, or the unforeseen changes in company policy and editorial submission guidelines, what is stated as fact at the time of this writing may become outdated or inapplicable later.

INTRODUCTION

A pescatarian diet is a flexible vegetarian diet that includes fish and other seafood. When you add fish to a vegetarian diet, you reap the following benefits:

Fish protein increases satiety as compared to beef and

chicken. This means you will feel full quickly and not

overeat. If you are looking to shed some pounds, it's the

right time to start being on a pescatarian diet.

Calcium is extremely important for your bone health. Merely eating vegetables does not provide your body with enough calcium. But adding fish to a vegetarian diet does

Fatty fish are great sources of omega-3 fatty acids. These acids help lower inflammation in the body, which, in turn, reduces the risk of obesity, diabetes, and heart disease.

Compared to other animal proteins, consuming fish contributes lesser to greenhouse gas emission. So, you can protect the environment and your health.

For some, just eating vegetables, fruit, and nuts can be boring. Adding fish or any other seafood helps improve the taste and overall mood of lunch and/or dinner.

Many people are allergic to eggs, lactose intolerant, or may want to avoid eating meat or dairy products. For them, fish can be a good source of complete protein, calcium, and healthy fats.

WHAT DO PESCATARIANS EAT?

SEAFOOD: Mackerel, bass, haddock, salmon, tuna, Hilsa, sardines, Pomfret, carps, cod, caviar, mussels, crayfish, oyster, prawns, lobster, crab, squid, and scallops.

VEGETABLES: Spinach, chard, radish greens, carrot greens, Bengal gram greens, beetroot, carrot, broccoli, cauliflower, cabbage, Chinese cabbage, sweet potato, radish, turnip, parsnip, kale, cucumber, and tomato.

FRUITS: Apple, banana, avocado, strawberries, blackberries, mulberries, blueberries, gooseberries, pineapple, papaya, dragon fruit, passion fruit, watermelon, muskmelon, guava, peach, pear, pluot, plum, and mango.

PROTEIN: Kidney beans, lentils, fish, mushroom, Bengal gram, sprouts, black-eyed peas, cowpeas, garbanzo beans, soybean, soy milk, edamame, and tofu.

WHOLE GRAINS: Brown rice, barley, broken wheat, sorghum, multigrain bread, and multigrain flour.

FATS & OILS: Olive oil, avocado oil, fish oil, ghee, sunflower butter, and rice bran oil.

Nuts & Seeds Almonds, walnuts, pistachios, macadamia, pine nuts, hazelnuts, sunflower seeds, melon seeds, pumpkin seeds, chia seeds, and flaxseeds.

Herbs & Spices Cilantro, dill, fennel, parsley, oregano, thyme, bay leaf, chili flakes, chili powder, Kashmiri red chili powder, turmeric, coriander, cumin, mustard seeds, English mustard, mustard paste, star anise, saffron, cardamom, clove, garlic, cinnamon, ginger, mace, nutmeg, Allspice, onion powder, garlic powder, and ginger powder.

BEVERAGES: Water, coconut water, detox" water>, and freshly pressed fruit/vegetable juices.

With these ingredients, you can easily come up with a diet plan that's nutritionally balanced. Take a look at this sample pescatarian diet plan.

SCALLOPS IN THE SHELL WITH ASIAN DRESSING

Servings:24

INGREDIENTS

- 2 teaspoons olive oil
- 1/2 onion, very finely chopped
- 2 garlic cloves, crushed
- 2 tablespoons sweet chilli sauce
- 2 teaspoons fish sauce
- 2 teaspoons palm sugar
- 1/2 cup (125ml) chicken or fish stock
- 24 scallops with roe on the shell
- Coriander leaves, to garnish

PREPARATION

1.In a small saucepan over low heat, heat the oil, then add the onion and cook for 2-3 minutes, or until soft. Simmer for 5 minutes, or until nearly all of the stock has been reduced, after adding the crushed garlic, sweet chili sauce, fish sauce, palm sugar, and stock. Delete from the equation.

2. Remove the scallops from their shells, clean them, and dry them with a paper towel. Cook the scallops for 1-2 minutes on each side in a pan or on the grill until they are cooked through. Return the shells to the pan, drizzle with a little sauce, and top with coriander leaves.

LINGUINE WITH SEARED SCALLOPS AND RICCADONNA ASTI SAUCE

Servings 2

INGREDIENTS

- 1 tbs olive oil
- 12 scallops, roe removed (optional)
- 10g unsalted butter
- 2 eschalots, peeled, thinly sliced
- 150ml Riccadonna Asti
- 160g fresh linguine
- 80g mascarpone cheese

- 1 tsp finely grated lemon zest, plus 2 tbs juice
- 2 tbs finely chopped chives

PREPARATION

1.Heat the olive oil in a big, heavy-bottomed frypan over high heat. Season the scallops with salt and pepper. When the pan is really hot, add the scallops and cook for around 15 seconds on each side, or until just opaque and seared on the outside. Delete from the equation.

2.Add the butter to the frypan and return it to medium heat. When the butter has melted, add the eschalots and cook, stirring constantly, for 2-3 minutes, or until softened but not coloured. Simmer for 5 minutes, or until the Riccadonna Asti has been reduced by a fifth. Delete from the equation.

3.Cook the linguine until al dente in a big pot of boiling salted water. In a separate cup, combine the mascarpone, zest, and juice, season with salt and pepper, and gently fold in the Riccadonna mixture. Drain the pasta and add it to the pan with the sauce, scallops, and any juices from the scallops. Toss to mix, then serve right away with chives on top.

STIR-FRIED NOODLES WITH CHICKEN ASPARAGUS AND OYSTER SAUCE

Servings 4

INGREDIENTS

- 2 x 200g packets egg noodles
- 2 tbs peanut oil
- 500g Lilydale Free Range Chicken Breasts, cut into thin strips
- 2 garlic cloves, crushed
- 1 tsp grated ginger
- 1 long red chilli, seeds removed, sliced

- 1 red onion, sliced
- 1 bunch asparagus, ends trimmed, cut into 5cm lengths
- 1/4 cup (60ml) oyster sauce
- 1 tbs soy sauce
- 1 tbs fish sauce
- 1/3 cup (80ml) chicken stock
- 3/4 cup coriander leaves, plus extra to garnish

PREPARATION

1.Cook the noodles as directed on the package, then drain and toss with 1 teaspoon of peanut oil.

2.In a wok, heat 1 tablespoon of the oil. Cook chicken in batches for 3-4 minutes, until golden and cooked through. Remove the object and set it aside.

3.Cook for 3-4 minutes, or until onion is soft and fragrant, in the remaining oil in the wok with the garlic, ginger, chili, and onion. Add the asparagus and cook for another minute, stirring constantly.

4.Return the chicken to the wok, add the sauces and stock, and cook for 1-2 minutes, stirring continuously, or until the sauce thickens. Toss in the coriander and noodles to heat up. Serve immediately with additional coriander leaves..

PRAWN FRIED RICE WITH OYSTER SAUCE

Servings 6

INGREDIENTS

- 1/3 cup (80ml) vegetable oil
- 4 eggs, beaten
- 2 bacon rashers, chopped
- 600g green prawns, peeled, deveined, roughly chopped
- 2 garlic cloves, crushed
- 1 tbs grated ginger
- 450g day-old cooked jasmine rice (3/4 cup uncooked)

- 2 tbs Chinese rice wine (shaohsing) or dry sherry
- 2 tbs oyster sauce
- Thinly sliced red chilli and spring onions sliced on an angle, to serve

PREPARATION

1.In a medium-high-heat pan, heat 2 tablespoons oil. Scramble the eggs for 1 minute or until cooked through, using a spatula. Remove the eggs from the pan and set them aside.

2.In the same pan, add the remaining 2 tablespoons of oil. Stir-fry the bacon for 4-5 minutes, before it starts to crisp, then add the prawns, garlic, and ginger and stir-fry for another 30 seconds. Stir in the rice, then add the rice wine and oyster sauce and stir to mix. Return the egg to the pan, season with a pinch of salt, and continue to stir-fry for 1 minute or until heated through, breaking the egg up as you go. Serve in a serving bowl with the chilli and spring onion on top.

OYSTERS WITH LEMONGRASS DRESSING

Servings 2

INGREDIENTS

- 1 lemongrass stem (white part only), outer layers discarded, finely chopped
- 1 teaspoon grated fresh ginger
- 1 long red chilli, seeds removed, roughly chopped
- 3 garlic cloves, roughly chopped
- 4 coriander roots (from a bunch of fresh coriander), roughly chopped
- 1/4 cup (60ml) white vinegar
- 1/4 cup (60ml) fish sauce

- 1/4 cup (60ml) lemon juice
- 2 tablespoons caster sugar
- 24 freshly shucked oysters
- Thinly sliced spring onion, soaked in iced water for 10 minutes, to garnish

PREPARATION

1.Blend the lemongrass, ginger, chili, garlic, coriander root, and vinegar until a thin paste develops in a blender or in a jug with a stick blender. Add the fish sauce, lemon juice, and caster sugar to the mixture in a cup. Whisk until the sugar is fully dissolved and the dressing is thoroughly mixed. Refrigerate until ready to use.

2.Place the oysters on serving plates, if desired, on a bed of rock salt to hold the oysters stable. Serve immediately after drizzling each with 2 teaspoons of the dressing and garnishing with spring onion..

SASHIMI OYSTERS

S

Servings 18

INGREDIENTS

- Crushed ice, to serve
- 18 freshly shucked oysters
- 100ml soy sauce
- 2 tablespoons pickled ginger
- 2 teaspoons wasabi paste

PREPARATION

1.Place the ice on a large platter and spread it out evenly. Add a little soy, a thin slice of ginger, and a dot of wasabi to the top of the oysters. Serve right away..

OYSTERS WITH LITTLE LEMON SANDWICHES

Servings 2

INGREDIENTS

- 1 thin-skinned lemon
- 12 freshly shucked oysters
- 4 slices thin wholemeal bread
- 1 tablespoon butter, softened

PREPARATION

1.Slice the lemon as thinly as possible after extracting the rind and pith. As you cut, remove and discard any seeds.

2.Place 2 slices of bread on a workbench and butter them evenly. Season with salt and pepper and layer with lemon slices. Remove the crusts from the remaining bread and cut into triangles. Serve the oysters with lemon sandwiches and a slice of black pepper.

SPICY CRAB BALLS WITH OYSTER SAUCE

Servings 6

INGREDIENTS

- 12 dried shiitake mushrooms
- 2 small red chillies, seeded, finely chopped
- 3 garlic cloves, crushed
- 250g raw fresh crab meat
- 300g minced pork
- 1 egg white, lightly beaten
- 1 tablespoon vegetable oil
- 2 onions, sliced
- 2cm piece ginger, cut into thin strips

- 1.25L (5 cups) fish stock
- 2 tablespoons oyster sauce, plus extra to serve
- 300g egg noodles, cooked
- 6 baby bok choy, halved, steamed
- Coriander, to garnish

PREPARATION

1.Bring a pot of water to a boil and soak the mushrooms for 10 minutes. Combine the lobster, fish, and eggwhite in a bowl with half of the chilli and two-thirds of the garlic. Season to taste, blend thoroughly, and roll into 18 balls. Refrigerate for 15 minutes after covering.

2.In a wide pan, heat the oil over low heat. Add the onion, the remaining chili and garlic, as well as the ginger.

3.Stir for 1-2 minutes, or until the vegetables are softened. Simmer for 5 minutes over medium heat with the stock and drained mushrooms. Simmer for another 5 minutes after adding the balls. Cook for another 2 minutes after adding the oyster sauce.

4.Assemble the noodles, bok choy, balls, and mushrooms in separate bowls. Finish with a drizzle of extra oyster sauce and a sprinkling of coriander..

SPICY MUSSELS WITH TOMATOES AND FENNEL

Servings 4

INGREDIENTS

- 1 tablespoon olive oil
- 1 red onion, thinly sliced
- 2 baby fennels, halved, thinly sliced
- 2 garlic cloves, thinly sliced
- 300ml white wine
- 400g can chickpeas, rinsed, drained
- 400g can chopped tomatoes
- 1 tablespoon tomato paste

- 1 teaspoon smoked paprika (pimenton), plus extra to serve
- 1kg pot-ready mussels
- 2 tablespoons coriander leaves
- Pinch of dried chilli flakes

PREPARATION

1.In a large saucepan, heat the oil over medium-high heat. Cook, stirring periodically, for 5 minutes or until onion, fennel, and garlic are softened. Bring to a boil with the white wine. Cook for 5 minutes, or until slightly reduced, after adding the chickpeas, tomatoes, tomato paste, and paprika.

2.Add the mussels to the pan, cover, and cook for 2 minutes on high heat. Give the pan a good shake and check the inside. Cover and cook for another minute if any mussels haven't opened yet. Any mussels that are still closed should be discarded.

3.In shallow bowls, divide mussels and sauce and top with coriander, chili, extra paprika, and black pepper..

LAKSA MUSSELS

S

Servings 4

INGREDIENTS

- 3 long red chillies
- 2 garlic cloves
- 2 lemongrass stalks (pale part only), roughly chopped
- 1 onion, roughly chopped
- 1 tsp ground coriander
- 1 tbs peanut oil
- 1 tbs brown sugar
- 1/2 cup (150g) laksa paste* (see Cook's Notes)
- 1 tbs fish sauce
- 400ml can coconut cream

- 3 cups (750ml) Massel Chicken Style Liquid Stock
- 1.25kg mussels, scrubbed, debearded
- 250g rice vermicelli noodles
- 1/2 bunch Thai basil* (see Cook's Notes), leaves picked
- 100g bean sprouts

PREPARATION

1 chilli, thinly sliced, set aside to serve. Remove the seeds from the remaining 2 chillies and halve them lengthwise in a food processor with the garlic, lemongrass, onion, and coriander. Pulse until the mixture resembles a paste.

In a large saucepan (with a lid), heat the oil until it shimmers, then add the chilli paste and cook for 2 minutes, or until fragrant. Cook for 3 minutes after adding the sugar and laksa paste.

Bring the stock, fish sauce, and coconut cream to a simmer, then cook for 5 minutes. Cover and cook the mussels for 3 minutes, or until they have all opened.

Meanwhile, in a heatproof tub, cover the noodles with boiling water and soak for 2 minutes. Drain and divide into four deep serving bowls.

To eat, ladle the laksa and mussels into cups, then top with basil, bean sprouts, and the reserved chilli..

MUSSELS WITH ALIOLI AND JAMON MIGAS

Servings 4

INGREDIENTS

- 2 tbs olive oil
- 1 cup torn day-old sourdough
- 50g jamon (Spanish cured ham), chopped
- 500g pot-ready mussels
- 1/3 cup (80ml) dry white wine
- Pinch of smoked paprika (pimenton)
- 2 tbs finely chopped flat-leaf parsley
- 1 eschalot, finely chopped
- ALIOLI
- 1 garlic clove, crushed

- 2 egg yolks
- 1/2 tsp Dijon mustard
- 1/2 tbs white wine vinegar
- Juice of 1/2 lemon
- 2/3 cup (165ml) each extra virgin olive oil and sunflower oil

PREPARATION

1.In a medium-sized frypan, heat the olive oil. Bread should be ground into crumbs, then added to the pan with the jamon and cooked for 2-3 minutes, until golden and crisp. Using a paper towel, absorb excess liquid.

2.In a food processor, mix the garlic, egg yolks, mustard, vinegar, and lemon juice for the alioli. Whising constantly, slowly pour in both oils in a thin steady stream until thick and pale. Season with salt and pepper and set aside.

3.In a big saucepan, heat the oil over high heat. Cover and cook mussels and wine for 3 minutes, or until mussels open. Transfer mussels to a bowl after removing them from their shells and reserving the shells and cooking liquid. Toss the mussels with 2 tablespoons alioli and 1/2 cup (125ml) strained reserved cooking liquid.

4.In a mixing bowl, combine the jamon crumbs, paprika, and parsley. Season with salt and pepper and set aside.

5. Fill mussel shells with mussels. alioli dressing, eschalot, and jamon crumbs on top.

MUSSELS WITH FREGOLA

S

Servings 4

INGREDIENTS

- 1kg mussels
- 2 tablespoons olive oil
- 1 red onion, halved, thinly sliced
- 2 garlic cloves, finely chopped
- 1 long red chilli, seeds removed (optional), thinly sliced on an angle
- 250g punnet cherry tomatoes, halved
- 2 tablespoons flat-leaf parsley leaves, plus extra chopped parsley to serve
- 200ml dry white wine
- 2 cups (500ml) fish or chicken stock

- 200g fregola (see Notes)

PREPARATION

1.Soak mussels for 1 hour in a big pot of cold water, adjusting the water twice (this helps remove any grit). Drain any broken shells and throw them out. Scrub the mussels thoroughly and cut the beards.

2.In a broad skillet, heat the oil over medium heat. Cook, stirring periodically, for 5 minutes or until the onion, garlic, and chili are soft.

3.Over medium-high heat, bring the tomatoes, parsley, and wine to a boil. Reduce the heat to medium-low and allow to simmer for 2 minutes before adding the mussels and covering with a lid. Cook for 2 minutes, shaking the pan occasionally, then remove any mussels that have opened and set aside. Cover and cook for another minute, then remove all the mussels and set them aside (discard any that haven't opened by then).

4.Return the pan to a low heat and add the fish or chicken stock, then add the fregola and cook for 15 minutes, or until tender.

5.Return the mussels to the broth, along with any juices, and heat through quickly, seasoning with sea salt and freshly ground black pepper if desired.

6.Distribute the mussels, fregola, and broth among four serving bowls, top with a sprig of parsley, and serve immediately..

MUSSELS COOKED IN ALE WITH GARLIC AND ESCHALOT

Servings 3

INGREDIENTS

- 1 tablespoon olive oil
- 20g unsalted butter, plus extra to serve
- 3 eschalots
- 5 garlic cloves, crushed
- 2 x 500ml bottles light ale
- Handful of flat-leaf parsley, finely chopped, plus extra to serve
- 1kg pot-ready mussels
- Seeded Irish brown bread, to serve

PREPARATION

1.In a large saucepan over low heat, warm the olive oil. Cook, stirring regularly, for 5 minutes, until onion is soft, adding butter, eschalots, garlic, and a pinch of sea salt flakes. Increase the heat to medium, add the beer, and cook for 5-6 minutes to infuse the flavors and cook off some of the beer. Cook for another 7 minutes, or until the mussels have opened, discarding the ones that are still closed.

2.Toss the mussels in a wide serving bowl with a generous amount of freshly ground black pepper, a small handful of finely chopped parsley, and buttered seeded Irish brown bread.

LEMONGRASS, COCONUT AND CHILLI MUSSELS

Servings 4

INGREDIENTS

- 2 teaspoons sunflower oil
- 1 lemongrass stem (pale part only), outer layer removed, finely chopped
- 2 long red chillies, seeds removed, thinly sliced lengthways
- 3cm piece ginger, peeled, thinly sliced
- 150ml light coconut milk
- 2 teaspoons fish sauce
- 1.25kg black mussels, scrubbed, debearded

- Coriander leaves, to serve
- 4 slices crusty bread

PREPARATION

1.In a large wok or saucepan, heat the oil over medium heat. Combine the lemongrass, chili, and ginger in a dish. Cook for 1 minute, stirring constantly, or until fragrant. Stir in the coconut milk and fish sauce until all is well combined. Boost the heat to high and bring to a boil.

2.Add the mussels, then cover with a tight-fitting lid in the wok or pan. Steam the mussels for 5 minutes, or until they open, shaking the pan periodically. Some mussels that haven't opened should be discarded.

3.Distribute the mussels among serving bowls, drizzle with some of the coconut broth, and top with coriander leaves. Serve alongside crusty bread..

STEAMED MUSSELS WITH AROMATICS

Servings 4

INGREDIENTS

- 2kg black mussels, scrubbed,debearded
- 1/2 leek (white and pale green part only), cut into matchsticks
- 1 carrot, cut into matchsticks
- 2 celery stalks, cut into matchsticks
- 2 garlic cloves, thinly sliced
- 2 bay leaves
- 2 thyme sprigs
- 1/2 cup (125ml) dry white wine
- 1/2 cup (125ml) thickened cream

- 1/4 cup flat-leaf parsley leaves

PREPARATION

1.Preheat the steamer oven to 100 degrees Celsius. In a metal pan wide enough to contain all of the mussels, combine the vegetables, garlic, bay leaves, and thyme. Preheat the oven to 200°F and bake for 2 minutes. Preheat the oven to 85°C, then add the mussels and wine to the pan with the vegetables and toss to combine. Cook for 12 minutes, or until mussels open (after this point, discard any that haven't opened).

2.Transfer mussels to a wide serving bowl with a slotted spoon and set aside. Return to the steamer for another minute to heat up, stirring cream into the cooking juices and seasoning to taste with salt and pepper. Bay leaves and thyme should be discarded. Serve the mussels with a dollop of cream and a sprinkling of parsley..

THAI MUSSELS WITH SWEET POTATO

Servings 4

INGREDIENTS

- 750g sweet potatoes, peeled
- 1.5kg black mussels
- 2 tablespoons vegetable oil
- 3 eschalots, finely sliced
- 3 garlic cloves, finely sliced
- 1 red chilli, finely sliced
- 2 tablespoons fish sauce
- 1 tablespoon sugar
- 3 tablespoons sweet chilli sauce

- Handful of basil leaves
- Handful of mint leaves
- Handful of coriander sprigs
- 2 tablespoons lime juice, plus 1 extra lime, cut into wedges
- Steamed white medium grain rice, to serve

PREPARATION

1.Cut the sweet potato into big chunks that are easy to eat. Cook for 10-15 minutes in a pan of salted water until tender, then drain.

2.Scrub mussels, remove beards, and discard those that do not close when tapped sharply.

3.In a heavy lidded pan over medium-high heat, heat the oil, eschalot, garlic, and chilli, along with 1 cup (250ml) water. Get the water to a boil.

4.Add the mussels, cover, and cook for a minute or two, shaking the pan periodically. Tongs may be used to remove any mussels that have opened and set them aside. Replace the lid and repeat the process, discarding any mussels that haven't opened after this time.

5.Heat the broth with the sweet potato, fish sauce, sugar, and chili sauce, stirring continuously.

6.Return the mussels to the pan once they've been opened. Toss in the herbs and lime juice thoroughly. Serve with lime wedges and steamed rice right away.

YELLOW CURRY MUSSELS WITH LIME

Servings 4

INGREDIENTS

- 1 tablespoon Thai yellow curry paste
- 2 cups (500ml) light coconut milk
- 3 teaspoons brown sugar
- Juice of 2 limes
- 2kg mussels, scrubbed, debearded
- 6 kaffir lime leaves
- 1 long red chilli, seeds removed, finely chopped
- 2 tablespoons coriander leaves, chopped

- 1 cup (200g) Doongara rice, cooked to packet instructions

PREPARATION

1.In a wok, combine the curry paste, coconut milk, sugar, and lime juice. Bring to a boil over high heat, stirring continuously, until the sugar has completely dissolved. Cover and add the mussels and lime leaves, if using. Cook for 5 minutes, or until all of the mussels have opened; discard any that haven't. Serve mussels and stock in bowls with rice and garnished with chilli and coriander..

BELGIAN MUSSELS

S

Servings 2

INGREDIENTS

- 1 tablespoon olive oil
- 1 celery stalk, thinly sliced on an angle
- 1 small leek (white part only), halved, sliced
- 2 garlic cloves, finely chopped
- 1 cup (250ml) low-carb beer
- 1 bay leaf
- 2 tablespoons lemon juice
- 6 thyme sprigs
- 1kg black mussels, scrubbed, debearded
- 1/4 cup chopped flat-leaf parsley
- 400g grainy bread, to serve

PREPARATION

1.In a broad skillet, heat the oil over medium-high heat. For 1 minute, cook celery, leek, and garlic until leek softens. Combine the beer, bay, juice, and thyme in a large mixing bowl. Get the water to a boil. Cook, covered, for 5 minutes, or until mussels open (discard any that don't). Apply the parsley and blend well. Serve with crusty bread..

MUSSELS, LEEK AND SAFFRON SOUP

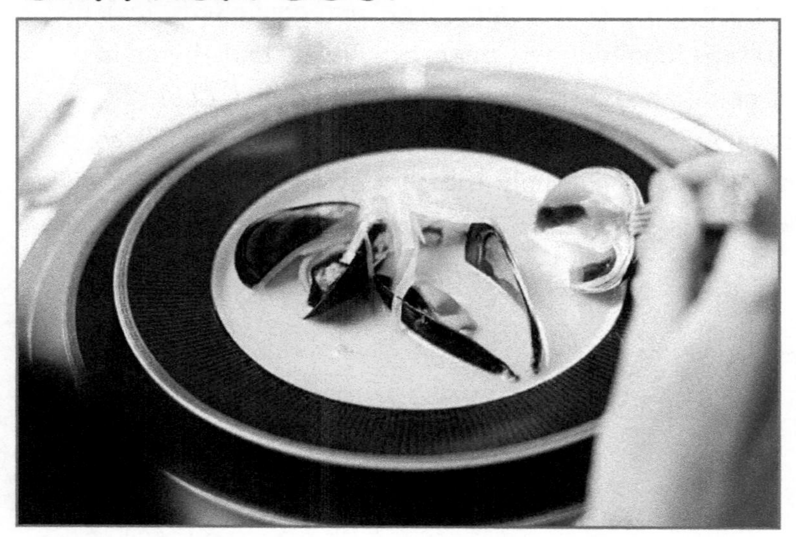

Servings 4

INGREDIENTS

- 1.5kg small mussels, scrubbed, beards removed
- 1/4 cup (60ml) dry white wine
- 2 leeks (white party only - to give about 450g)
- 75g unsalted butter
- 1 small onion, finely chopped
- 2 tbs plain flour
- 450ml good-quality fish stock*
- Good pinch of saffron threads
- 50ml thickened cream

PREPARATION

1.In a big pan, combine the mussels and wine. Cover and cook for 2-3 minutes over high heat, shaking the pan occasionally, until the mussels open; discard any mussels that do not open after this time. Place them in a colander set over a bowl to catch the liquid and set aside to cool. Remove the mussels from all but eight of the most attractive shells, and set them aside until ready to eat.

2.Cut one 5cm-long piece of the white portion of the leek into matchsticks. Chop the remaining ingredients finely. In a medium-low-heat pan, melt the butter, then add the chopped leeks and onion and cook for 3-4 minutes, until soft but not browned.

3.Stir in the flour and cook for 1 minute on low heat. Stir in the strained mussel liquid and stock gradually, then bring to a boil, stirring continuously. Reduce the heat to low and leave the saffron to simmer for 25 minutes.

4.In the meantime, place the leek matchsticks in a pan of boiling salted water, return to a boil, drain, and rinse under cold running water. Remove from the oven and set aside until ready to eat..

BEN'S BAKED MUSSELS PROVENCALE

Servings 6

INGREDIENTS

- 2 tablespoons olive oil
- 30 large mussels, scrubbed, debearded
- 3 garlic cloves
- 1/2 cup (125ml) dry white wine
- 4 small eschalots, finely chopped
- 4 anchovy fillets, chopped
- 4 vine-ripened tomatoes, blanched, peeled, seeds removed, finely chopped
- 1/2 dried red chilli, chopped

- Juice of 1 lemon, plus wedges to serve
- 350g rock salt
- HERB CRUST
- 4 slices stale bread, crusts removed
- 2 teaspoons thyme leaves
- 1/4 cup each of flat-leaf parsley leaves, tarragon leaves and chervil sprigs
- Finely grated rind of 1 lemon

PREPARATION

1.In a food processor, finely grind the crust ingredients and set aside.

2.In a broad skillet, heat 1 tablespoon of oil over high heat. Add the mussels, 1 garlic clove cut, and the juice. Cook, covered, for 2-3 minutes, until mussels open, shaking occasionally (discard any unopened after this time). Remove from heat and strain the liquid, reserving it. Remove the mussels' top shells and loosen the meat.

3.Preheat the oven to 200 degrees Celsius.

4.Heat the remaining oil in a wide pan and cook the eschalots for 3-4 minutes, stirring occasionally, until tender. 2 minutes later, finely cut the remaining 2 garlic cloves and return to the pan with the anchovies. Cook for 2-3 minutes after adding the tomato and chili. Using a fine sieve, strain the mussel liquid (except the last 1-2 teaspoons, which contain the most grit) and add 1 cup to the pan. Bring to a boil, then reduce to a low heat and continue to cook for 10 minutes, stirring occasionally, until slightly thickened. Season with salt, pepper, and lemon juice to taste.

5.In a large ovenproof serving dish, spread the salt and arrange the mussels on top. Fill shells halfway with sauce, then top with crumbs. Preheat oven to 350°F and bake for 5 minutes, or until crust is crisp. Serve with lemon wedges on the side.

KAFFIR LIME LEAF AND COCONUT MUSSELS

Servings 4

INGREDIENTS

- 1 tbs sunflower oil
- 2 eschalots, finely chopped
- 2 garlic cloves, chopped
- 4 kaffir lime leaves,
- 2 thinly shredded
- 1 tbs grated ginger
- 2 tsp palm sugar or brown sugar, grated
- 2 tsp fish sauce
- 400ml can coconut milk

- Juice of 1 lime
- 1kg pot-ready mussels
- 3 small red chillies, thinly sliced
- 375g dry wheat noodles, cooked according to packet instructions
- 1 bunch coriander, leaves picked

PREPARATION

1.In a large saucepan with a lid, heat the oil over medium heat. Cook eschalot for 2-3 minutes, stirring occasionally, until softened. Cook for 1-2 minutes, until fragrant, with the garlic, whole kaffir lime leaves, and ginger. Put to a boil the palm sugar, fish sauce, coconut milk, and lime juice. Cover with a lid and add the mussels. Cook for 2-3 minutes, shaking the pan periodically, until the mussels have opened. Stir in the chilli.

2.Ladle the mussels and liquid over the noodles in a deep serving bowl. To eat, garnish with coriander and shredded kaffir lime leaves.

STEAMED MUSSELS WITH COCONUT AND LEMONGRASS

Servings 4

INGREDIENTS

- 2 tablespoons olive oil
- 3 garlic cloves, crushed
- 1 onion, thinly sliced
- 2 stalks lemongrass, bruised
- 1 tablespoon thin ginger strips
- 1 small leek, washed, cut into thin strips
- 1 carrot, cut into thin strips
- 4 celery stalks, cut into thin strips
- 1 teaspoon mild curry powder

- 1kg mussels, washed, bearded
- 300ml white wine
- 1L fish stock
- 200ml coconut milk
- 100ml cream
- 2 tablespoons chopped fresh coriander

PREPARATION

1. In a frying pan over low heat, heat the oil and then add the garlic, onion, lemongrass, ginger, leek, carrot, and celery. Cook for 5 minutes, then stir in the curry powder for 30 seconds to release the flavors. Place the chicken on a plate and set it aside.

2.In a large saucepan, combine the mussels, wine, and stock. Cook for 5 minutes with the lid on. Move mussels to cups, throwing out those that haven't opened. Reduce the coconut milk and cream in the pan by half. Cook for 2 minutes after returning the vegetables to the sauce, then mix in half of the coriander.

3.Remove the lemongrass and discard it, then ladle the sauce over the mussels and top with the remaining coriander.

SALMON WITH THAI-STYLE DRESSING

Servings 4

INGREDIENTS

- 250g packet rice stick noodles
- 1/3 cup (80ml) sweet chilli sauce, plus extra to serve
- 1/2 cup (125ml) lime juice
- 1 tablespoon fish sauce
- 2 tablespoons finely chopped coriander leaves, plus extra leaves to garnish
- 1/2 cup finely chopped mint leaves
- 1 teaspoon grated ginger

- 1 teaspoon grated garlic
- 4 x 150g skinless salmon fillets
- 1 tablespoon vegetable oil
- Chopped peanuts, to garnish
- Finely sliced red chilli, to garnish

PREPARATION

1.In a large mixing bowl, combine the noodles and cover with boiling water. Allow for a 5-minute soak.

2.In a mixing bowl, combine the sweet chilli, lime juice, fish sauce, basil, garlic, and ginger with 1/2 cup warm water. To mix, stir all together.

3.Preheat a chargrill or grill to high heat. Cook for 2 minutes on either side, or until salmon is just cooked through, brushing with oil.

4.Rinse and drain the noodles before tossing with half of the dressing. Place on plates, top with salmon, and drizzle with the rest of the dressing. Serve with extra coriander, peanuts, and chili on the side.

SALMON TEMPURA WITH TWO DIPPING SAUCES

Servings 6

INGREDIENTS

- 2 eggs
- 150ml sparkling mineral water, chilled
- 3/4 cup (115g) plain flour
- 1/3 cup (55g) cornflour
- 1 tablespoon finely sliced kaffir lime leaves
- Sunflower oil, for deep-frying
- 500g skinless salmon fillet, cut into 1cm strips
- Baby Asian greens, to garnish (optional)
- HONEY AND SOY DIPPING SAUCE

- 2 teaspoons honey
- 2 teaspoons toasted sesame seeds
- Juice of 1 lime
- 1 tablespoon sesame oil
- 1 tablespoon soy sauce
- 2 teaspoons grated ginger
- 2 spring onions, finely chopped
- 1 tablespoon chopped coriander leaves
- CHILLI DIPPING SAUCE
- 2 red chillies, halved, seeds removed
- 1 garlic clove
- 2 coriander roots
- 2cm piece grated ginger
- 30g palm sugar, grated
- 1/2 cup (125ml) lime juice
- 1 tablespoon fish sauce

PREPARATION

1.In a mixing bowl, combine all of the ingredients for the honey and soy sauce. Delete from the equation.

2.Pulverize the chilli, garlic, coriander, and ginger in a mortar and pestle to produce the chilli sauce. Stir in the palm sugar, lime juice, and fish sauce, then set the mixture aside.

3.In a mixing cup, whisk together the eggs and mineral water. Add the flours and stir with chopsticks until just combined; the batter should be lumpy. In a small mixing bowl, gently fold in the kaffir lime leaves.

4.Heat an oil-filled deep-fryer or a large heavy-bottomed saucepan to 190°C. (If you don't have a deep-fryer thermometer, measure a cube of bread; when the oil is hot enough, it will turn golden in 30 seconds.) Dip the salmon in the batter and fry in batches for 2-3 minutes, or until golden and crisp. Using a paper towel, absorb excess liquid.

5.Spread out on a platter and season with salt. If using, garnish with baby Asian greens and serve with dipping sauces..

WHOLE SALT-BAKED SALMON WITH SOTT'OLIO AND

Servings 8

INGREDIENTS

- 3-4kg rock salt
- 2 tablespoons fennel seeds
- 2 tablespoons black peppercorns
- 2kg whole salmon
- 2-3 lemons, halved
- 1/2 bunch parsley stalks
- 2 fennel bulbs, roughly sliced (fronds reserved for garnish)
- SOTT'OLIO

- 500g freshly podded peas (or frozen)
- 500g shelled broad beans, peeled
- 100ml good-quality extra virgin olive oil
- 10 mint leaves
- 15-20 basil leaves
- Zest of 1 lemon
- TARRAGON MAYONNAISE
- 2 egg yolks
- 1 teaspoon English mustard
- Juice of 1/2 lemon
- 100ml good-quality extra virgin olive oil
- 20 tarragon leaves

PREPARATION

1.Preheat the oven to 170 degrees Celsius.

2.In a mixing bowl, combine the salt, fennel seeds, and peppercorns. In a baking tray wide enough to accommodate the fish comfortably, make a 1cm-deep layer of the salt mixture (about half). Place the fish in the center of the tray on the salt. Stuff the lemons, parsley stalks, and fennel bits into the cavity of the fish. Cover with the remaining salt and pat down to ensure that it is uniformly dispersed around the fish. Remove the fish from the oven after 20-30 minutes, or before the salt crust has hardened. Keep in mind that the salt will be extremely hot. Allow 30 minutes for preparation.

3.In the meantime, make the sott'olio. Blanch the peas and broad beans for 5 minutes in boiling salted water, drain, and then put in a bowl with enough oil to fully cover them. Tear herbs and combine with lemon zest in a mixing bowl. Season with salt and pepper to taste, then stir to mix.

4.To make mayonnaise, in the bowl of a food processor, combine the yolks, mustard, lemon juice, salt, and pepper and process until smooth. While the motor is working, slowly drizzle in the oil until the mixture thickens, then add the tarragon leaves and pulse to combine.

5.Ladle the sott'olio onto the plates. Remove the crust and skin from the fish, then put the bits on the sott'olio. Top with mayonnaise and the fennel fronds you saved.

POACHED SALMON WITH BEURRE BLANC SAUCE AND

Servings 2

INGREDIENTS

- 2 x 200g salmon fillets, skin-on, pin-boned
- 1/2 cup (125ml) milk
- 4 black peppercorns
- 1/2 cup flat-leaf parsley leaves, roughly chopped, stalks reserved
- 80g dried egg fettuccine

- 1 vine-ripened tomato, seeds removed, finely chopped
- 1 tablespoon olive oil
- BEURRE BLANC SAUCE
- 1/4 cup (60ml) dry white wine
- 2 teaspoons lemon juice
- 2 tablespoons thin cream
- 60g cold unsalted butter, finely diced

PREPARATION

1.Preheat the oven to 180 degrees Celsius.

2.Add the milk, black peppercorns, reserved parsley stalks, and 2 teaspoons sea salt to the salmon fillets in a small baking dish, then pour in enough water to come halfway up the sides of the salmon fillets. Cover with foil and bake for around 20 minutes, or until salmon fillets are cooked to your preference.

3.Cook fettuccine until al dente in a saucepan of boiling salted water, then drain. Toss the parsley leaves, tomato, and olive oil with the pasta in a cup, seasoning with sea salt and black pepper to taste.

4.In the meantime, reduce the white wine to 1 tablespoon in a small saucepan over medium heat to create the beurre blanc sauce. Simmer for 1 minute after adding the lemon juice and cream. As the liquid continues to boil, whisk in the butter, a few bits at a time, until completely mixed. Remove the pan from the heat and pour the mixture into a serving jug.

5.Transfer the salmon fillets from the poaching liquid to the serving plates with a large fish slice and a drizzle of beurre blanc sauce.

6.Serve the salmon separately from the fettuccine and the remaining sauce.

SALMON WELLINGTON

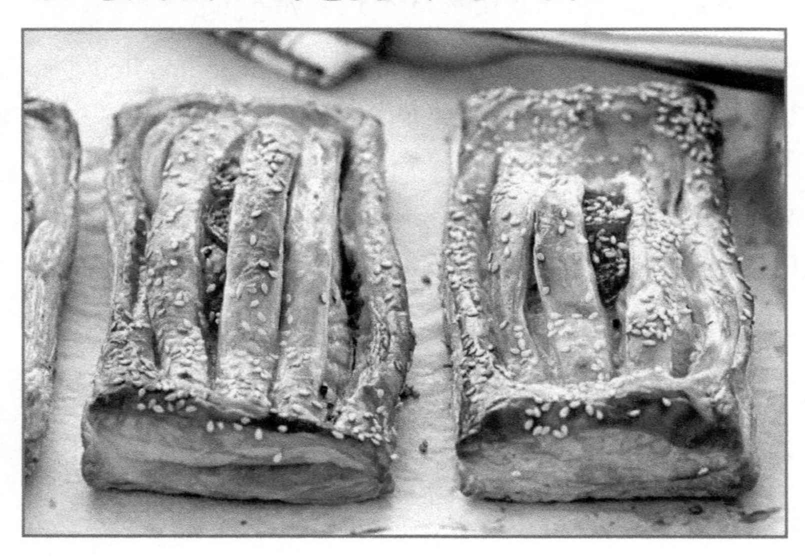

S

Servings 4

INGREDIENTS

- 4 sheets frozen puff pastry, thawed
- 2 tablespoons basil pesto
- 4 x 100g skinless salmon fillets
- 4 cherry tomatoes, thinly sliced
- 1/3 cup (80ml) lemon juice, plus extra wedges to serve
- 1 egg, beaten
- 1 tablespoon sesame seeds

PREPARATION

1.Preheat the oven to 200 degrees Celsius. Using baking paper, line a baking tray.

2.Cut each sheet of puff pastry in half. 2 teaspoons pesto in the center of 4 sheets of puff pastry, leaving a 3-4cm pastry border Season each with salt and pepper and a salmon fillet. Top each salmon fillet with alternating tomato slices. Brush the pastry border with beaten egg and drizzle with lemon juice.

3.In the center of the remaining 4 pastry bits, cut 4-5 long slits. Place each piece of puff pastry over a salmon fillet, gently pulling to separate the strips, then press down the edges and trim to turn each parcel into a tidy rectangle. Brush the pastries with beaten egg and sesame seeds on both sides.

4. Carefully raise the parcels onto the prepared baking tray with a fish slice, and bake for 20-25 minutes, until the fish is just cooked through and the pastry is puffed and golden. If desired, serve with lemon wedges and a green salad..

SALMON RILLETTES WITH BAGEL TOASTS

Servings 8

INGREDIENTS

- 450g skinless salmon fillet, pin-boned
- 125g unsalted butter, softened
- 6 eschalots, very finely chopped
- 1 tablespoon creme fraiche
- 250g smoked trout fillet
- 2 tablespoons lemon juice
- 1 tablespoon extra virgin olive oil
- 2 egg yolks
- 2 tablespoons Pernod (optional)
- 1 tablespoon chopped dill, plus a sprig to garnish

- Clarified butter, to top
- BAGEL TOASTS
- 2 large bagels or 4 mini bagels
- Olive oil, to brush
- 1 garlic clove, halved

PREPARATION

1.Drizzle 1 tablespoon of sea salt over the salmon fillet in a shallow bowl. Refrigerate the salmon fillet for 1 hour, rotating it once.

2.Preheat the oven to 350°F. Line a steamer with baking paper, then steam the salmon fillets for 8 minutes over a saucepan of simmering water, until only cooked but still slightly opaque in the middle. Remove the salmon from the pan and set it aside to cool.

3.In a medium-sized frypan, melt 40 grams of butter. Cook, stirring constantly, for 2 minutes, or until the eschalots are soft. Cook for another 2 minutes after adding a pinch of salt.

4.In a mixing bowl, beat the remaining 85g of butter with hand beaters until pale. Mix in the creme fraiche thoroughly. Connect the eschalots, lemon juice, oil, egg yolks, Pernod (if using), and dill to the bowl with the steamed salmon and smoked trout. Season well after gently mixing until the mixture is mixed but still coarse. Cover with a 1cm layer of cooled clarified butter in a glass bowl or clip-lock container wide enough to hold the entire mixture. Chill for at least 1 hour after adding the dill sprig. (The rillettes will keep in the fridge for 3 days.

5.Preheat the oven to 180°C for the bagel toasts. Make two half-rings out of the bagels or mini-bagels, then thinly slice them. Brush with olive oil and rub with the cut side of the garlic clove on a baking tray in a single layer. Allow to cool after baking the bagel slices for 2-3 minutes until golden. (The bagel toasts will keep for 3 days in an airtight container.)

PASTA WITH SMOKED SALMON IN VODKA AND

Servings:4

INGREDIENTS

- 120g unsalted butter
- 1 large leek, thinly sliced
- 3/4 cup vodka
- 2 tablespoon lime juice
- 1 teaspoon lime zest
- 150g smoked salmon, sliced

- 2 tablespoons Aristocrat capers, drained and chopped
- 250ml thickened cream
- Salt and freshly ground black pepper, to taste
- 1 red chilli, drained and thinly sliced (If desired)
- 500g cooked pasta
- Fresh parsley leaves, torn
- Freshly chopped green onions

PREPARATION

1.In a large skillet, melt the butter and sauté the sliced leek until slightly golden. Combine the vodka, juice, and zest in a mixing glass. Simmer for a moment. Reduce the temperature.

2.Combine the sliced salmon, capers, and cream in a mixing bowl. Simmer for a few minutes. Season with pepper, salt, and chili to taste.

3.Toss in your favorite cooked pasta and top with parsley and green onions.

SWEET SOY TUNA WITH GREEN TEA NOODLES

Servings:4

INGREDIENTS

- 4 tablespoons soy sauce
- 4 tablespoons mirin
- 4 tablespoons sake
- 1 tablespoon palm sugar
- 1 tablespoon grated fresh ginger
- 2 garlic cloves, crushed
- 4 (about 130g each) tuna steaks
- 200g packet green tea noodles
- 1 teaspoon sesame oil

- 1 tablespoon toasted sesame seeds
- Wasabi, to serve

PREPARATION

1.In a ceramic bowl, combine the soy sauce, mirin, sake, sugar, ginger, and garlic. Set aside the tuna steaks for 30 minutes to marinate, turning once.

2.Cook the noodles according to the package instructions, then drain and rinse with cold water. To avoid the noodles from sticking together, move them to a bowl and toss with sesame oil.

3.Preheat a chargrill plate or a barbecue. Add the tuna when it's really hot, reserving the marinade. Sear for 1 minute on each side. Set aside for a while to relax.

4.Heat the marinade in a pan over low heat for 2 minutes, or until it is fully warm.

5.Ladle boiling water over the noodles in a colander. Return to the bowl and toss in half of the warm marinade.

6.To serve, divide the noodles among serving plates, top with the tuna, and drizzle with the remaining marinade. Serve with sesame seeds and wasabi as a garnish..

SEARED SESAME TUNA

S

Servings:6

INGREDIENTS

- 3 (about 300g each) tuna steaks
- 3 1/2 tablespoons soy sauce
- 3 tablespoons sesame seeds
- 1 1/2 tablespoons peanut oil, plus extra to fry
- 2 handfuls of rocket or baby spinach leaves
- 1 small Spanish red onion, cut into rings
- 1 1/2 tablespoons sherry vinegar
- 1 teaspoon sesame oil

PREPARATION

1.Drizzle two tablespoons soy sauce over the tuna. Refrigerate for 1/2 hour after pressing sesame seeds into both sides of the fish.

2.Heat a small amount of peanut oil in a pan over high heat and fry the tuna for around 1 minute on one hand, then flip and cook for another half minute. Set aside for a while to relax.

3.In the meantime, combine the remaining ingredients in a mixing bowl and move to a serving plate. Place six diagonal slices of each steak on top of the salad.

LINGUINE WITH CHILLI TUNA AND BROCCOLINI

Servings:4

INGREDIENTS

- 2 bunches broccolini, roughly chopped
- 500g linguine
- 370g canned tuna in chilli oil
- 1/4 cup (60ml) olive oil
- 3 garlic cloves, thinly sliced
- 1/2 cup basil leaves
- 1 teaspoon dried red chilli flakes
- 1/3 cup (35g) finely grated parmesan

PREPARATION

1.Cook broccolini for 2 minutes in a big pot of boiling salted water.

2.Remove with a slotted spoon, then cook pasta according to package directions in the same water.

3.In the meantime, drain the tuna and set aside 2 tablespoons of the chili oil. In a deep frypan over medium heat, heat the chili and olive oils, then add the garlic and cook for 1 minute, or until fragrant. Cook for another 10 seconds after adding the basil.

4.Take the pan off the heat and throw in the broccolini. Stir in the tuna gently so that no bits of tuna are broken up.

5.In a large mixing bowl, remove the pasta. Toss in the tuna mixture, chili flakes, parmesan, and season with salt and pepper to taste. Before eating, gently toss to mix.

BEAN AND TUNA SALAD

S

Servings:4

INGREDIENTS

- 2 x 185g tuna in olive oil
- 200g French or thin green beans
- 250g canned cannellini beans, rinsed
- 2 1/2 tablespoons chopped flat-leaf parsley
- 1 red onion, thinly sliced
- 1/4 cup (60ml) lemon juice
- Grated zest of 1 lemon
- 1 tablespoon lemon pepper (see note)
- 2 garlic cloves, crushed
- 1 teaspoon Dijon mustard
- 1 tablespoon olive oil

- 1 bunch rocket leaves, trimmed, washed
- 2 hard-boiled eggs, finely chopped

PREPARATION

1.Reserve the oil after draining the tuna. Blanch the French beans for 1 minute in boiling salted water before rinsing in cold water.

2.Toss together the French beans, tuna, cannellini beans, 1 tablespoon parsley, and onion in a big mixing bowl. Toss thoroughly.

3.In a separate cup, season the lemon juice, zest, lemon pepper, garlic, and mustard with salt. Slowly drizzle in the tuna oil and olive oil, whisking constantly. Seasoning should be tested.

4.Drizzle the dressing over the bean mixture, then toss in the rocket leaves. Place the salad on serving plates and top with the reserved parsley and egg..

TUNA, LEMON AND ROCKET RISOTTO

Servings:4

INGREDIENTS

- 2 x 185g cans tuna in oil with chilli
- 1 small onion, chopped
- 1 1/2 cups (375ml) fish stock
- 350g arborio risotto rice
- 100ml white wine
- 1/4 cup grated parmesan
- Zest and juice of 1 lemon, plus extra zest to serve
- 50g wild rocket

PREPARATION

1.Flake the tuna to separate it, reserving 1 tablespoon of the oil.

2.Heat the tuna oil in a heavy-bottomed saucepan over medium heat and cook the onion for 1-2 minutes, or until softened.

3.Combine the fish stock and 1 1/2 cups (375ml) water in a mixing bowl. Cook for 2-3 minutes, stirring constantly to ensure that the rice grains are evenly coated. Enable the alcohol to evaporate before adding the wine.

4.After the wine has been consumed, add the diluted stock a ladleful at a time until all of the liquid has been absorbed, about 20 minutes.

5.When the rice is finished, add the tuna, parmesan, and lemon rind and juice, and season with salt and pepper to taste. Serve on a bed of rocket with extra zest on top.

TUNA AND RISONI SALAD

S

Servings:4

INGREDIENTS

- 1 cup risoni pasta
- 1/2 cup (120g) fresh ricotta
- 1 tablespoon chopped basil, plus 1/4 cup small leaves
- 2 tablespoons olive oil
- 2 tablespoons capers, rinsed, drained
- 2 small tomatoes, seeds removed, cut into thin wedges
- 2 cups wild rocket leaves
- 1/4 cup (60ml) lemon juice

- 2 x 185g good-quality canned tuna in springwater, drained

PREPARATION

1.Cook the risoni according to the package instructions in a saucepan of boiling, salted water. Drain and rinse well with cold water.

2.In a small mixing bowl, combine the ricotta, chopped basil, and 1 tablespoon olive oil. Season with salt and pepper to taste.

3. In a large mixing bowl, combine the cooked pasta, basil leaves, capers, tomato, rocket leaves, lemon juice, and the remaining tablespoon of olive oil. Mix in big chunks of tuna gently, taking care not to split them up too much.

4.Serve with a spoonful of ricotta on top.

TUNA BRANDADE

S

Servings:4

INGREDIENTS

- 2 large potatoes (about 500g)
- 1 cup (250ml) reduced-fat milk
- 2 garlic cloves, crushed
- 1 eschalot, finely chopped
- 185g can good-quality tuna in springwater
- 1 tablespoon white wine vinegar
- 1/4 cup (60ml) olive oil
- 1/3 cup roughly chopped dill sprigs
- Crostini, to serve
- Niçoise olives, to serve
- Rocket, to serve

PREPARATION

1. Peel the potatoes and cut them into 1.5cm cubes. Bring to a boil in a saucepan with the milk, garlic, and eschalot. Reduce to medium-low heat and cook for 8-10 minutes, or until the potato is tender.

2.Remove the pan from the heat and drain the tuna before adding it to the potato mixture. With a fork, gently mash the potatoes, leaving some larger chunks. Stir together the vinegar, oil, and half of the dill sprigs.

3.Serve the brandade with the rocket, olives, and the remaining dill on crostini.

TUNA ON TURKISH TOAST

S

Servings:2

INGREDIENTS

- 185g can tuna slices, drained
- Soft goat's cheese
- 1 slice of marinated eggplant
- A few rocket leaves
- Some thinly sliced red capsicum

PREPARATION

1.From a Turkish loaf, cut two sandwich pieces. Top each sandwich with 1 slice of marinated eggplant, a few rocket leaves, tuna slices, and thinly sliced red capsicum, then crumble soft goat's cheese over the base.

TUNA SPAGHETTI

S

Servings:1

INGREDIENTS

- 250g spaghetti
- 185g can tuna slices, drained
- 2 tsp grated lemon zest
- 1tsp capers
- 1 small, finely chopped tomato (seeds removed)
- A handful of baby spinach

PREPARATION

1. 250g spaghetti, cooked according to product directions Return to the hot pan after draining.

2.Combine tuna, 2 teaspoons grated lemon zest, 1 teaspoon capers, a pinch of dried chili flakes, 1 small finely chopped tomato (seeds removed), and a handful of baby spinach leaves in a mixing bowl. To mix, gently toss all together.

ASPARAGUS AND TUNA

S

Servings:2

INGREDIENTS

- 10-12 fresh asparagus spears
- 185g can tuna slices, drained
- Decorate with rocket, shaved parmesan and green peppercorns

PREPARATION

1. Place 10-12 spears of fresh asparagus on serving plates. Arrange the tuna on top of the asparagus. Toss

with rocket, shaved parmesan, and green peppercorns before serving (in jars from supermarkets).

TUNA AND BASIL PIZZA

S

Servings:2

INGREDIENTS

- 170g jar marinated artichoke hearts, drained
- 2 anchovy fillets
- 2 garlic cloves
- 1/4 cup (60ml) olive oil
- 1/3 cup basil leaves, plus small leaves to garnish
- 1 large pizza base (preferably wood-fired)
- 2 cups grated mozzarella
- 185g can tuna slices, drained
- 1/4 red onion, very thinly sliced
- 1/4 cup small black olives

PREPARATION

1.Preheat the oven to 200 degrees Celsius.

2.In a food processor, puree the artichokes, anchovies, garlic, olive oil, and basil until smooth.

3.Spread the basil paste over the pizza base on a pizza tray. Half of the mozzarella cheese is sprinkled on top, followed by the tuna slices. Sprinkle the remaining mozzarella cheese and black olives over the red onion.

4.Bake the pizza for 10-12 minutes, or until the base is crisp and the cheese has melted. Serve with small basil leaves as a garnish.

TUNA SLICES WITH AVOCADO AND CAESAR DRESSING

Servings:4

INGREDIENTS

- 2 garlic cloves
- 1 anchovy fillet
- Juice of 1 lemon
- 3 drops Worcestershire sauce
- 1/2 cup light whole-egg mayonnaise
- 2 tablespoons grated parmesan
- 2 avocados

- 185g can tuna
- 1 tablespoon finely chopped flat-leaf parsley leaves

PREPARATION

1.In a food processor, mix the garlic, anchovies, lemon juice, Worcestershire sauce, mayonnaise, parmesan, and 2 tablespoons water. Process until a loose dressing forms.

2.Cut the avocados in half and remove the stones. Fill each avocado half halfway with tuna, then drizzle with dressing and parsley.

PEPPER AND FENNEL-CRUSTED TUNA WITH FIGS

Servings:4

INGREDIENTS

- 1 tablespoon fennel seeds
- 720g sashimi-grade piece tuna fillet
- 2 tablespoons olive oil
- 8 small figs, quartered
- 5 cups mizuna* or wild rocket
- 1/4 cup (60ml) lemon juice
- Lemon wedges, to serve

PREPARATION

1.Combine fennel seeds, 2 teaspoons coarsely ground black pepper, and 1 teaspoon sea salt in a tray. Trim the tuna and cut it in half lengthwise to make two long logs. Coat the bits in the fennel mixture all over, then cover and set aside for 10 minutes at room temperature.

2.In a wide frypan, heat 1 tablespoon of the oil over high heat. When the pan is really hot, add the tuna and cook for 3 minutes, rotating once to brown all sides. On the outside, the tuna should be seared, and the middle should be rare.

3.In a mixing bowl, combine the figs, mizuna or rocket, lemon juice, and the remaining tablespoon of oil.

4.Thinly slice the tuna and toss it into the salad. Serve with lemon wedges on the side.

TUNA CEVICHE WITH AROMATIC SALAD

Servings:4

INGREDIENTS

- 3 cups of loosely packed leaves including frisee (smaller inside leaves), cress, purple basil, mint & basil
- 1 bunch coriander, leaves picked
- 500g fresh tuna, cut into 1cm slices
- 2 avocados, peeled, diced
- 1 teaspoon lemon juice
- 50ml vegetable oil
- MARINADE
- Juice of 5 limes

- 1 teaspoon sesame oil
- 1 teaspoon grated palm sugar
- 1 teaspoon soy sauce
- 1 teaspoon coconut milk
- GARNISH
- 150ml vegetable oil
- 100g red Asian eschalots, finely sliced
- 3 garlic cloves, finely sliced

PREPARATION

1.To make the marinade, combine all of the ingredients in a ceramic cup.

2.Heat the oil in a small frypan for garnish. Separately fry the eschalots and garlic until golden. Using a slotted spoon, remove the chicken, drain on paper towels, cool, and set aside.

3.Place the leaves and herbs in a bowl, cover, and refrigerate until needed.

4.Coat the tuna slices in the marinade to make sure they are fully covered. Enable 5 minutes to pass.

5.Salt and pepper the avocados, then toss with lemon juice.

6.Drain the tuna gently and place it on a serving tray. Drizzle a little oil on top of the avocado. Toss the remaining oil with the salad and herb leaves, then put on top of the avocado.

7.In a mortar and pestle, crumble fried eschalots and garlic with 1/2 teaspoon salt and 1/2 teaspoon sugar. Serve immediately with a sprinkle of salt and pepper on top of the salad.

TUNA-STUFFED CAPSICUM (GLUTEN-FREE)

Servings:4

INGREDIENTS

- 2 large red capsicum, halved, seeds and membrane removed
- 1 tablespoon olive oil
- 425g can tuna in oil, drained
- 2 hard-boiled eggs, chopped
- 1 tablespoon capers, chopped
- 2 tablespoons chopped chives
- 5 tablespoons (100ml) good-quality mayonnaise
- 200g wild rocket
- 1/3 cup (80ml) good-quality French dressing

PREPARATION

1.Preheat the oven to 180 degrees Celsius.

2.Place the capsicum cut-side up on a baking tray, drizzle with oil, and roast for 15 minutes. Remove and set aside to cool.

3.In a mixing bowl, combine the tuna, egg, capers, and half of the chives. Season with salt and pepper and enough mayonnaise to tie.

4. When the capsicums are cool enough to handle, fill the cavities with the tuna mixture.

5.Toss salad leaves with half of the dressing and serve with capsicum on serving plates. Drizzle with the remaining dressing and top with the chives. Add salt and pepper to taste..

QUICK VITELLO TONNATO (VEAL WITH TUNA SAUCE)

Servings:4

INGREDIENTS

- 4 (about 200g each) veal chops
- 1 garlic clove, crushed
- 2 tablespoons olive oil
- 185g can tuna in oil
- 2 anchovies
- 6 capers
- 2 tablespoons lemon juice
- 1/2 cup mayonnaise
- 1/4 cup picked parsley leaves

BEAN SALAD

- 410g can 4-bean mix
- 1/2 red onion, finely chopped
- 1 tomato, seeds removed, finely chopped
- 1 tablespoon chopped flat-leaf parsley
- 2 tablespoons olive oil
- 1 tablespoon red wine vinegar

PREPARATION

1.To make the bean salad, add all of the ingredients in a mixing bowl, season to taste with salt and pepper, and stir to combine. Delete from the equation.

2.Salt and pepper the veal after rubbing it with garlic. In a wide frypan over high heat, heat the oil and fry the veal for 3-4 minutes on each side (the veal should still be pink in the centre). Enable chops to cool after removing them from the sun.

3.In a food processor, puree the tuna, anchovies, capers, lemon juice, mayonnaise, and parsley until smooth. Serve a veal chop on each plate with a side of bean salad and sauce.

STIR-FRIED RICE WITH CHILLI TUNA

Servings:4

INGREDIENTS

- 350g brown medium grain rice (or use 4 cups leftover cooked rice)
- 2 tablespoons olive oil
- 8 bacon rashers, rind removed, diced
- 1 garlic clove, crushed
- 1 cup fresh or frozen peas
- 210g can tuna in chilli oil, drained
- 1/2 cup spring onions, finely sliced, plus extra to serve

- 1/4 cup (60ml) light soy sauce, plus extra to serve

PREPARATION

1.Cook rice until al dente in salted boiling water, then drain and refresh.

2.In a wok over high heat, heat the oil, then add the bacon and fry until crisp. Remove the pan from the heat and drain on kitchen paper.

3.In a wok, stir-fry the rice and garlic for 1 minute before adding the peas, tuna, spring onions, cooked bacon, and soy sauce. Stir-fry easily until thoroughly heated.

4.Garnish with extra soy sauce and spring onions before serving.

TUNA WITH CAPER AND OLIVE SALSA

Servings:4

INGREDIENTS

- 20 semi-dried tomatoes
- 4 tablespoons (1/3 cup) salted baby capers, rinsed
- 12 black olives, pitted, sliced
- 1/4 cup chopped flat-leaf parsley
- 1 long red chilli, seeds removed, thinly sliced
- 2 tablespoons lemon juice
- 1/3 cup (80ml) extra virgin olive oil, plus extra to brush
- 4 x 125g tuna steaks

- 100g baby salad leaves
- Lemon wedges, to serve

PREPARATION

1.To make the salsa, mix the tomatoes, capers, olives, parsley, and chili in a bowl. Set aside 2 tablespoons of the lemon juice and olive oil, season with salt and pepper, and apply the remainder to the salsa mixture. Toss all together.

2.Preheat a chargrill pan or a nonstick frypan to high heat. Brush tuna with a little oil and sear for 1-2 minutes on each side on a hot grill. (Make sure it's still rare in the middle; once removed from the sun, it'll continue to cook.)

3.Divide each tuna steak into three to four sections. Toss the remaining salad leaves with the remaining dressing and divide among four plates. Toss in the tuna and split the salsa among the dishes. If needed, garnish with lemon wedges.

CROSTINI WITH TUNA, OLIVES AND CAPERS

Servings:3

INGREDIENTS

- 1/2 wood-fired loaf or ficelle, thickly sliced on the diagonal
- 1/4 cup (60ml) olive oil
- 2 garlic cloves
- 125g pitted black olives, cut into slivers
- 1 tablespoon salted capers*, rinsed,
- 8 semi-dried tomatoes, chopped
- 1 tablespoon chopped fresh oregano
- 125g can smoked tuna slices, drained

- 1 cup (about 50g) wild rocket

PREPARATION

1.Preheat the oven to 180 degrees Celsius. 1 tablespoon oil, brushed on bread slices Bake for 8 to 10 minutes on a baking sheet (or toast on a chargrill). While the bread is still sweet, halve a garlic clove and rub the cut side over it.

2.Finely chop the remaining garlic and combine with the olives, capers, tomatoes, and oregano in a mixing bowl. Add the tuna, breaking it up if it's too high. Place a few rocket leaves on each slice of bread, then pile on the toppings and drizzle with olive oil.

FATTOUSH WITH SUMAC-SPICED TUNA

Servings:4

INGREDIENTS

- 2 Lebanese pita bread rounds, split
- 2 small Lebanese cucumbers, peeled, halved lengthways
- 2 vine-ripened tomatoes, halved
- 1/2 red capsicum, seeds removed
- 4 small radishes, sliced
- 6 spring onions, sliced
- 1/2 cup roughly chopped flat-leaf parsley
- 1/4 cup roughly chopped mint

- 1 tablespoon ground sumac or cumin
- 4 (about 115g each) small tuna steaks
- 1 tablespoon extra virgin olive oil
- DRESSING
- 1/4 cup (60ml) olive oil
- 2 tablespoons lemon juice
- 1 garlic clove, crushed
- 1 teaspoon ground cinnamon
- 1 tablespoon ground sumac or cumin

PREPARATION

1.Preheat the grill to medium and cook the split pita bread rounds for 1 minute on each side, or until golden and crisp. Put aside the crumbled crisp bread in tiny shards.

2.Cucumber seeds should be scooped out and discarded. Remove the seeds and juice from the tomatoes and discard them. Cucumber, peppers, and capsicum should be chopped and combined with radishes, spring onions, parsley, and mint.

3.Combine the olive oil, lemon juice, garlic, cinnamon, and sumac or cumin in a mixing bowl to make the dressing. Put aside after seasoning.

4.For the tuna, on a plate, combine additional sumac or cumin, sea salt, and freshly ground black pepper, and press one side of the tuna into it. In a frypan, heat the oil and sear the tuna, spice-side down, for 2 minutes until golden, then flip and cook for 1 minute on the other side, leaving the center yellow. Remove from the oven and set aside for 5 minutes before cutting into 2cm bits.

5.Drizzle the dressing over the salad, crisp pita bread, and tuna and serve right away.

TUNA AND OLIVE TAPENADE TOASTS

Servings:6

1 focaccia or ciabatta

INGREDIENTS loaf

- 1 garlic clove, halved
- 3-4 tablespoons olive oil, plus extra to brush
- 1 teaspoon dried oregano
- 1 1/3 cups (200g) good-quality kalamata olives, pitted
- 95g can tuna in oil, drained
- 4 anchovy fillets

- Pinch dried chilli flakes
- 1 tablespoon salted capers, rinsed
- 1 tablespoon Dijon mustard
- 1 tablespoon lemon juice
- Boiled quail eggs, to serve

PREPARATION

1.Preheat the oven to 160 degrees Celsius.

2.Thinly slice the focaccia or ciabatta and rub with the garlic clove's cut side. Drizzle with extra virgin olive oil and season with dried oregano.

3.Preheat the oven to 350°F and toast the slices for 5-7 minutes on each side, until crisp.

4.In a food processor, combine the olives, salmon, anchovies, chili, capers, mustard, and lemon juice. Season with pepper, then mix in a food processor.

5.While the motor is working, drizzle in the olive oil in a slow, steady stream until a rich, dark paste forms. The tapenade can keep in the fridge for up to a week if kept sealed. Serve the tapenade with the crisp toasts and, if desired, quail eggs.

CONCLUSION

PROVIDES OMEGA-3 FATTY ACIDS

One of the main reasons fish is so good for us is because it contains high levels of omega-3 fatty acids. In a world where most people consume far too many omega-6 fatty acids from refined vegetable oils, salad dressings, and processed spices, increasing omega-3 foods is urgently needed.

Omega-3 fatty acids act as a counterbalance to omega-6 fats and help keep inflammation down by balancing the levels of omega-3 and omega-6 fatty acids. Omega-3 fatty acids are considered to be anti-inflammatory, while omega-6 fatty acids are anti-inflammatory. We need both types, but many people lack omega-3 fatty acids. Consuming higher omega-3 levels has been linked to better mental health, lower triglyceride levels, improved reproductive health and fertility, better hormone control, and a lower risk of diabetes.

HELPS IN LOWERING INFLAMMATION

The reason the omega-3s found in fish are so valuable is mainly because of their ability to fight inflammation. They help control inflammatory diseases that lead to numerous diseases, including cancer, rheumatoid arthritis, and asthma.

Both types of polyunsaturated fats described above play an important role in the body and contribute to the formation of our hormones, cell membranes and immune

responses. But omega-3 and omega-6 fatty acids have opposite effects when it comes to inflammation. In general, too much omega-6 and too little omega-3 cause inflammation. Inflammation is believed to contribute to the development of chronic conditions like cancer, diabetes, heart disease, and more.

PROMOTES HEART HEALTH

EPA and DHA are two omega-3 fatty acids that are essential for controlling inflammation and promoting heart health. Studies show that daily consumption of EPA and DHA can help reduce the risk of heart disease and death from heart disease, sometimes as effective as prescription drugs like statins. The combination of nutrients in seafood also helps regulate the heartbeat, lower blood pressure and cholesterol, reduce blood clot formation, and lower triglycerides. All of these can help protect against heart disease and stroke.

CAN HELP PROTECT AGAINST CANCER

Research shows that eating more fish and seafood high in omega-3s benefits the immune system and helps fight cancer by suppressing inflammation. While a vegetarian diet has been linked to a lower incidence of certain types of cancer (such as colon cancer), pescatarianism is associated with an even lower risk compared to vegetarians and non-vegetarians, according to some studies.

Several studies also suggest that consuming plenty of omega-3 fatty acids may help those previously diagnosed with cancer by stopping tumor growth. A pescatarian lifestyle high in omega-3s can also help people undergoing chemotherapy or other cancer treatments, as they help maintain muscle mass and regulate inflammatory responses that are already compromised in cancer patients.

COMBATS COGNITIVE DECLINE

Omega-3 fatty acids like DHA are vital for proper brain development and maintenance of cognitive function in old age. Many studies have shown that low omega-3 levels in the elderly are linked to several markers of impaired brain function, including dementia or Alzheimer's disease. Lower omega-3 levels during pregnancy have even been linked to children who have lower memory test scores and learning difficulties.

BOOSTS THE MOOD

Because they fight oxidative stress, which affects the proper functioning of the brain, the omega-3s from fish and seafood have been linked to better mental health and a lower risk of dementia, depression, anxiety, and ADHD. This means that a Pescatarian diet can be a natural anti-anxiety remedy and help manage the symptoms of ADHD while fighting off symptoms of depression.

SUPPORTS WEIGHT LOSS

Many people have started using the Pescatarian diet for weight loss, and for good reason. Low intake of omega-3

fatty acids has been linked to obesity and weight gain. Studies also show that people who eat more plant-based foods (including vegetarians) tend to have lower BMIs and better weight management, probably because they eat more fiber and fewer calories.

Not only that, but healthy proteins and fats are critical to feeling full, and many of the nutrients found in fish can help reduce cravings. Regardless of your diet, aim for a high intake of fruits, vegetables, high quality proteins, healthy fats, seeds, nuts, fiber, and phytochemicals. All of these can help you lose weight quickly and keep it off.

Lightning Source UK Ltd.
Milton Keynes UK
UKHW020806250521
384334UK00001B/190